PERFECTION
to a FAULT

A Small Murder
in Ossipee, New Hampshire
-1916-

PERFECTION
to a FAULT

A Small Murder
in Ossipee, New Hampshire
-1916-

JANICE S. C. PETRIE

SEATALES PUBLISHING COMPANY

Second Printing: May 20, 2016

ISBN 10: 0970551088
ISBN 13: 978-0970551085

ACKNOWLEDGMENTS

There are several people and organizations who helped to bring this book together. I would like to thank Mr. Barry Hill of the Ossipee Historical Society, Ms. Jane Lyman of the Concord State Library, and staffs of the Carroll County Courthouse, *The Boston Globe*, and John Hancock Mutual Life Insurance for locating information imperative for the accurate depiction of this history. I would like to thank my parents, whose intriguing stories of the small cottage on the shore of Lake Ossipee and captivating accounts of the crime that took place there sparked my curiosity and motivated me to write this book. This book is dedicated to Mike, Kristen, and David, whose inspiration and support made this endeavor possible.

Here's to soaring with the eagles!

COVER DESIGN:
MELLARIUM CREATIVE
MELLARIUMCREATIVE.COM

Contents

I. PRESENCE

The simple cottage didn't possess the ominous appearance Joe Foley had expected as he surveyed the property from across the street. Joe always thought that a lakefront cottage on the shores of Lake Ossipee, New Hampshire, would be out of reach financially, and couldn't believe his good fortune as he eyed the prime real estate. When a friend who worked with Joe at the "Good Gulf" Oil Company in Boston approached him with news of the unbelievable deal he could get on a cottage just 140 miles north of Boston, Joe jumped at the chance. Joe always enjoyed a bargain, and the property was actually in fairly good shape. His friend was very candid in explaining why this cottage was such a buy, when similar lakefront cottages in 1955 were being appraised for far more than an asking price of $2,300. But the fact that some poor woman was murdered in the cottage at the turn of the century was of little interest to Joe. A bargain held far more weight for Joe than a memory, whether pleasant or horrific.

"Spare me the details," Joe was heard to say, and the papers were passed within the week.

Although Joe knew of the history of the cottage, he felt that it was nobody's business but his own, and this was especially true when it came to making any revelations to his new and somewhat skittish wife, Anna. What Joe didn't count on was the fact that the rest of the local folk in Ossipee knew all about the history of the cottage, and didn't mind sharing their knowledge with others. This became evident when Anna walked into the general store in Ossipee, to pick up a few odds and ends she had forgotten to pack from Dorchester that morning.

In 1955, Dorchester was a nice but modest neighborhood on the south side of Boston. From a Dorchester perspective, only the rich had country cottages to escape the sweltering, summer heat of the city. Thus, when short and stout Anna traipsed into Ossipee's general store dressed in her bright shift, she had the air of someone of status, of grandeur, and of regality. When she assembled her items to be purchased on the checkout counter, the clerk noted she was strange to the community. The conversation that ensued went something like this:

"You're new around these parts, aren't you?"

"Ya, I'm from Dorchester. My husband bought a cottage just around the corner from here on Pine Shore Road," Anna replied.

"Not number 60?!" interjected a customer who couldn't contain her curiosity while eavesdropping on the conversation.

Anna turned to face the woman. "That's the one," said Anna, with a note of apprehension in her voice. She couldn't imagine why this woman, who was a total stranger to her, should sound so alarmed.

The clerk quietly snickered while the customer revealed to Anna the nature of her husband's recent purchase. "I can't believe anyone would be interested in buying that place where such a dastardly thing happened. We heard that someone from down Boston way bought the old cottage. Guess the only people they could sell that place to were outsiders. No one around here would take the gift of it."

"What are you talking about?" Anna questioned, genuinely concerned by the woman's remarks, unable to imagine what she could possibly mean.

"Murder, that's what I'm talking about. Some poor, mousy woman from down your way in Boston was murdered in that cottage. Surely, you must have known!" the woman declared quite unsympathetically.

Anna gasped, and turned to Joe, who had just entered the store. She studied Joe's face for a sign that the woman was mistaken. Anna found no comfort in Joe's expressionless features.

"Do you know anything about this?" Anna shrieked. Anna was known for her shrill voice, and now, being fairly agitated, Anna's voice was as piercing as a siren.

"We ought to be running along," Joe said quietly, to nobody in particular, totally ignoring his wife's outburst. Joe had already guessed the topic of conversation that had just taken place, and felt it better to avoid a heated argument. He didn't wish for his personal matters to become the latest subject of gossip in this small town.

"Are these bags ours?" Joe asked the clerk. The clerk nodded and turned to the next customer in line, anticipating an altercation and glad he wasn't standing in Joe's shoes.

Joe struggled to lift the heavy sacks of groceries, for Joe was a somewhat tall, but slender man, whose muscles had long since given way to his sedentary lifestyle. Joe's tank top shirt and chino pants drooped down around his aging body—a sharp contrast to his wife's rotund physique.

"Is it true?" Anna asked, furious now for his deception. "How could you buy the place and not tell me?!"

"I'll explain on the way home," Joe said calmly as he walked out of the store, leaving Anna to storm out after him.

Although Anna was too hysterical to have listened to answers that might have been forthcoming to her questions, it didn't matter. Joe knew nothing more about the background of the cottage than Anna had just found out. And neither Joe, nor Anna, were educated in the art of research. After all, ignorance, especially in this situation, really was bliss. The couple decided they would never stay at the cottage alone, especially at night.

This was not a hard pact to carry out, because their extended family was so large. Anna and Joe's marriage had occurred in mid-life—a second marriage for both of them. Joe's first wife, who also happened to have been Anna's only sister, had been dead for years. Anna's first husband had deserted her years ago, leaving her with four children to raise by herself. Anna's four children, plus Joe's four children, all grown, added up to eight families, some with children of their own, to come to Ossipee and enjoy the beautiful lakeside cottage with them. Joe and Anna really never were alone, and the cottage served the whole extended family well. Nobody in the family, save Anna and Joe, knew of the cottage's history, since Joe had convinced Anna that no good would come from others knowing the story about a murder that happened at least forty years ago.

During the summer of 1956, Anna's eldest son, Steve, and his wife, Thelma, spent an occasional Saturday afternoon at the Ossipee cottage with their two children, Ron and Jan, aged three years and fifteen months, respectively. Steve was a good-looking man with chestnut hair and sky blue eyes. Although he wasn't overly tall, his body was toned from a full summer's swimming. Thelma's dark brown hair and eyes and her slight size and figure were a perfect complement to Steve's build. They made a striking couple. When August approached and Steve mentioned he would be reserving his regular cottage at Deer Cove on Lake Ossipee for one week in the month, Joe and Anna insisted that their cottage would be vacant during the week. They maintained that it would be silly for Steve to stay anywhere else. After many objections, Steve found it was easier to accept their hospitality, even though he enjoyed the Deer Cove area more.

And so it was decided. Steve and Thelma arrived on a Saturday morning, unpacked their groceries, and joined many of Steve's brothers and sisters, as well as stepbrothers and stepsisters, for a day of fun. This day was spent the way many families would spend their time at a lakeside cottage. Children kept busy making mud pies on the dock, swimming, and catching sunfish, while many of the adults accompanied Steve for a spin in his boat. The barbecue was immense, with chicken, hamburgers, hot dogs, potato salad, and corn on the cob. Nobody went away hungry. When dusk approached, one by one, each family headed for home. Joe and Anna were the last to leave. Joe wanted to show Steve how to turn the water off at the old fieldstone foundation and how to secure the cottage until their next visit. As the last few families left, Thelma had a sinking feeling in the pit of her stomach. There was an unmistakably cold, damp feeling in the old cottage that she hadn't noticed before. She tried to shake these feelings of discomfort, understanding that she was probably just a little lonely. She reasoned the feeling away by acknowledging that many people feel lonely after enjoying a fun afternoon. When the festivities had ended, and the people she enjoyed had left, it was quite normal to feel a little let down. But this seemed much stronger than a simple let down.

Steve walked into the cottage armed with an old radio and a .22 rifle, feeling he was ready for anything the wilds of New Hampshire had to offer. The oversized cast iron stove in the kitchen would have kept the cottage nice and warm on a typical cool August night in Ossipee. However, this was not a typical night. The Ossipee area had been experiencing a balmy August, and despite its mountainous setting, the air temperature remained warm and comfortable throughout the summer evenings. Thus, the wood that was neatly stored at the side of the stove was not regarded as a necessity for the week's stay.

Perhaps Steve and Thelma's initial feelings of discomfort resulted from their chance meeting of an old man who came staggering down the road just about sunset. As he made his way down the path, a swarm of flies encircled his head, attracted by the stench of a body that hadn't been bathed for weeks. The patches of dirt on his leathery face were somewhat hidden by the stubble of his beard. They waved as they watched him head down the dirt road and into the woods, where he was apparently spending the night. They turned and headed inside, Steve eyeing his rifle that was propped against the kitchen wall. Feeling the bullets he had thrown in his pocket that morning, having given little serious consideration to actually using them, Steve now wondered if he should load his weapon.

Perhaps these feelings were partly a product of the musty stench that intruded upon the fresh, pine scented air. The fieldstone floor in the cellar would become saturated with water from the lake, especially in the spring, when the water level in the basement would rise to two or three feet. The cellar was never totally dry, and the presence of mold and mildew seemed unavoidable. The dirt road that led to the cottage was often rendered impassable in the spring by the rising water that fed Lake Ossipee. Even with all of the windows opened wide, the musty smell didn't fully vanish.

Perhaps their discomfort was magnified by the fact that each room in the cottage was darkened by the tall pine trees surrounding the house. The shadeless, curtainless windows left one feeling exposed to the outer darkness when interior lights were on in the evening. The only finished room in the cottage was the kitchen, which was paneled with boards of knotty pine. The rest of the rooms contained exposed studding, with no insulation in the walls. The breezes outside were often felt inside, as they filtered through the cracks in the siding. The lack of sheet rock or paint, combined with the occasional appearance of a cobweb or two, added to the character of the cottage.

Perhaps it was the fact that Thelma and Steve were accustomed to living in the city and suburbs, and the quiet of the place was so unlike the environment they were accustomed to, that it seemed strange to only hear the lonely cries of the loons on the lake, the chirping of the crickets, and the croaking of bullfrogs. Stale air filled with the faint scent of exhaust had become second nature to them, and the sounds of traffic and neighborhood children playing in the streets had created a sense of hominess. This quiet wilderness was a new experience, one that was enjoyed while friends and family were around, but was replaced with a sense of melancholy in their absence. Whatever the reason, as they walked through the front door of the cottage that night, they felt an uncontrollable chill take over their bodies.

Steve and Thelma looked at their son, asleep on the couch in the living room.

"All this fresh, clean Ossipee air has done our son in!" said Steve, trying to ignore his feelings of apprehension.

"Ron didn't stop all day, and I've never seen him eat so much," Thelma stated in a matter-of-fact manner, clearly indicating her mind was elsewhere.

Steve walked over to Ron and slid his arms underneath him, lifting his limp body, and carrying him into one of the spare bedrooms. It was nearly pitch black outside now, and Steve made the rounds of the cottage, closing and locking each window, despite the warmth of the summer evening. As he entered the master bedroom, Steve peaked into the crib where Jan was sleeping, then quietly tiptoed out of the room.

"The house is all secure, windows and doors are locked, and children asleep," Steve called to Thelma, as he passed through the kitchen threshold.

Steve put his arms around Thelma, and whispered in her ear, "Are you up for some gin rummy?" This was hardly Steve's usual choice of activities on those rare occasions when he found himself alone with his wife, with both children fast asleep. But Thelma was relieved, because she still hadn't lost her sense of uneasiness in the old cottage.

Thelma hunted for a piece of paper and a pencil, while Steve tried to locate a deck of cards. They hadn't bothered to bring a deck from home, since they knew that Joe and Anna were avid Whist players, and usually had several decks from which to choose. Joe and Anna would always partner up, and when the score wasn't going their way, Anna would throw the cards down on the table and insist upon playing with a new deck. Steve finally found a spare deck in a kitchen drawer.

"There's no paper in this G.D. kitchen!" Thelma cried, with an unusual strain in her voice.

"Well, look in one of the other rooms. There's got to be a pad of paper somewhere around here. How else would Joe and Mom keep a record of all their winning scores!" Steve was used to being beaten by Joe and Anna on a regular basis.

Thelma rushed over to her pocketbook and pulled out an old electric bill envelope and a pen and slapped it on the table.

"This will have to do," she said, sitting down at the table.

Steve began to deal the cards. Thelma picked up each card in turn and placed it in the proper position in her hand. Then she paused for a moment to listen and said, "Are you sure all of the windows are locked?"

Steve welcomed this comment as a chance to check once again himself. A chill had settled into the room, and he wondered if he had missed a window. Steve made the rounds once more without any protest. As he opened the front door to check the lock from the outside to be sure it was working properly, a warm breeze blew past him into the cottage. Stepping outside, Steve felt a mild, comfortable breeze gently blowing off the water, and his anxiety was almost instantaneously whisked away. Feeling better, Steve closed the door and locked it, noticing the chill within the cottage once more. Although Steve felt far safer outside the cottage, he thought this would never make sense to Thelma, and returned to the kitchen without mentioning his strange discovery.

Steve turned the old radio dial to the local station in Ossipee, where they were broadcasting the Republican convention. The presidential race was unusually interesting this time, not because Eisenhower was seeking reelection, because he was extremely popular at the time, both with the Republican and Democratic parties. However, there was a large movement to remove Richard Nixon as running mate, and an offer of a cabinet post was made directly from the President's advisors. But Nixon wouldn't hear of it, and announced in April that he would remain as Eisenhower's running mate. Four weeks before the Republican national convention was to begin, an announcement was leaked to the press that with Nixon as a running mate, Eisenhower would lose six percent of the vote. However, Nixon remained on the ballot.

As the convention was broadcast from San Francisco, the political speeches seemed to have a warming effect in the old kitchen. Thelma and Steve became relaxed and actually began to enjoy their card game. Herbert Hoover spoke of preserving personal liberties but portrayed the country in an optimistic, positive light. By the time the crowd had finished giving Hoover a ten-minute ovation, Steve had won one game of gin, leaving Thelma with a two-game lead.

Thelma and Steve were joking and laughing while the keynote speaker, Governor Arthur B. Langlie, pointed out that the Eisenhower administration had achieved so much in such a short period of time. For the first time since everybody had left, Steve and Thelma were relaxed and enjoying their vacation.

Then suddenly, an hysterical, yet muffled scream came from the bedroom where Ron was sleeping. Steve and Thelma were on their feet in an instant, only to find Ron sobbing from underneath the covers, his head and arms struggling to free themselves from his bedding. His feet were writhing on the pillow at the other end of the bed, cold from exposure to the chilly room. In Ron's considerably short life thus far, he had always been a tranquil sleeper, never even attempting to untuck his bed. It was difficult to believe he had turned his body around under the covers. Thelma pried Ron lose from his bedding and clutched him to her chest. His face was damp and reddened from the tears and sweat that ran down the sides of his cheeks. Thelma spoke soothingly to her son as she shot a questioning expression Steve's way in search of an explanation. Steve had none to offer.

"Maybe we should all sleep together tonight," Steve said quietly.

"Let's leave," Thelma's eyes pleaded with Steve's, as they suddenly welled up with tears.

"We can't leave now," said Steve, after entertaining the idea for a moment. "The boat is in the lake and it's too dark for me to drag it onto the trailer to take it home. And the water has to be turned off outside at the foundation. I wouldn't feel right about leaving the place without securing it properly. It just wouldn't be right. We'll all go to bed right now, together. We'll put the kids in bed between us, and as soon as day breaks we'll leave, I swear."

Thelma sighed and walked back into the kitchen to clean up the table, carrying Ron in her arms, trying to settle him down. As she placed the cards in one of the kitchen drawers, Thelma felt a disquieting apprehension grow with the prospect of staying in the cottage for the rest of the night. When Steve walked into the kitchen after checking on the baby, Thelma confronted him once more about remaining in the cottage.

"Let's sleep in the car. It's a station wagon. There's room enough," Thelma pleaded, trying to remain as rational as she could.

But Steve remembered the vagrant in the woods, and didn't feel he could guarantee his family's safety under those conditions.

"We really have to stay the night. We'll leave the windows open. That awful chill doesn't seem to stay in the rooms where the windows are open, don't you think?" Steve glanced at Thelma for what he hoped would be a reassuring nod, but Thelma just turned her eyes from him and walked to the bedroom, still holding Ron in her arms. She laid her son down on the bed, covering him with a sheet and crawled into bed next to him, fully clothed. The crib holding the baby was between the bed and the wall, and Jan was still sleeping. Steve opened the window and laid down on the edge of the small, double mattress beside Thelma. Soon the room filled with a fresh pine aroma carried in on a warm, twilight breeze. However the essence of the cottage had not changed with the air. Steve and Thelma got little sleep that night, drifting off for fifteen or twenty minutes at a time, then abruptly waking with a feeling of inexplicable urgency.

Thelma opened her eyes and looked at the clock on the dresser across the way. It was 4 A.M. She laid quietly, contemplating her surroundings. Ron shifted restlessly from his right side to his left and moaned in his sleep. The warm breeze had subsided, replaced by the tense chill of the room. Realizing the sun would be rising soon, Thelma crawled toward the foot of the bed and began packing the family's suitcases. Her uneasiness about staying in the cottage had not diminished, even with the first glimpse of sunrise reflecting off the mirror-like surface of the lake.

"We have to leave this cottage now," Thelma asserted, waking Steve from what was probably his longest stretch of sleep that night. Thelma lifted the baby from the crib and began to change her diaper. Steve rubbed his eyes with the back of his hand and gently nudged his son awake.

"Come on, Ron. Time to get up," Steve whispered, realizing the irony of him waking his son so early in the morning. Usually, it was the other way around. Steve sat on the edge of the bed and thought about the meager two weeks vacation he was given each year. He sighed, "Well, this is the start of a vacation to remember."

"It will get better," Thelma assured him. "I think I have everything now. Come on, Ron, let's go get in the car."

Thelma closed and buckled the suitcase. She took Ron by the hand, as she picked the baby up and balanced her on her hip. When Thelma bent down with her free hand to reach for the suitcase, Steve quietly said, " I'll get that for you. Give me fifteen minutes and I'll have the water shut off and the boat loaded onto the trailer, OK?"

"I'll be in the car with the kids waiting for you," Thelma said in relief.

"Are you sure you won't be more comfortable waiting in here? You could get some cereal or a muffin while you wait. I'm a little hungry, and it's about a three-hour ride home." Steve didn't want to admit to himself the possibility there may really have been something wrong with the old cottage—something that couldn't be described to another human being who hadn't experienced the peculiar evening. After all, there was no proof—no physical injuries to his family or to the cottage to back up his story. Nobody would understand their misgivings about the cottage.

I. Presence

Thelma just slowly shook her head and left the cottage, never turning back to get one more glimpse of the old place. Steve was as good as his word and in record time Steve, Thelma, Ron, and Jan, with the boat in tow, were headed down old Pine Shore Road, bouncing in and out of dusty ruts as they went along. They left the town of Ossipee, never to return to that cottage again.

Not wishing to upset his mother, Steve never mentioned the events of the night's stay to Joe or Anna. He simply returned the key, stating that Thelma and he had decided to take day trips for the rest of the week instead. The steady flow of cloth diapers were easier to handle with the modern convenience of a washer and dryer. They hadn't anticipated how hard it would be to hand wash and line dry all of the baby's things. Joe and Anna bought the story, and thus neither couple was forced to reveal the secrets they held.

Within a year, Joe sold the cottage to Anna's youngest son, Bob, who made a decent income renting the old place on a weekly basis to vacationers. However three years later, Bob sold the cottage to a man for $3,500, who remodeled the ill-fated dwelling before moving in. Many say the old place looked pretty sharp after its new face-lift. However, the sturdy fieldstone foundation of the old cottage remained the same. It was the original foundation that had been built by the famous and respected mason, Mark Winkley, so many years before, when the cottage was new.

II. THE TRAGEDY

It is a radiant morning on the shores of Lake Ossipee. There is a hint of autumn in the air, and although the trees that line the lake shores have not totally begun to turn to brilliant pallets bursting with color, their reflection mirrored in the sapphire waters is nonetheless breathtaking. Although the tract of land is the same one where Joe and Anna spent their summer in 1956; the date is September 28, 1916, a time when everybody's eyes have turned to the events of World War I, even in the sleepy town of Ossipee. Joe and Anna are merely teenagers growing up on the south side of Boston; and the cottage on Ossipee Lake, as many of the locals call it, is owned by Florence Arlene and Frederick L. Small.

The Smalls had moved to the two-story cottage just three years earlier, most likely impressed by its panoramic view of the White Mountain region of New Hampshire. Frederick Small was a stock broker from Massachusetts, and retained many of his business connections from the Boston area, despite the distance of his current residence. Florence Arlene Curry and Frederick Small were relative newlyweds when they arrived in Ossipee, having married two years earlier. The couple had originally met at Florence's family's farm in Southborough, Massachusetts, shortly before their marriage. For the most part, the pair kept to themselves, with the exception of an occasional evening card game with a neighboring couple. Because Frederick enjoyed tinkering, he would help out a cottage owner when the need arose to run a telephone wire or fix an outboard motor.

Because Frederick was very handy, he was able to make many attractive additions to his lakefront home, which he originally purchased for $900. One of the most substantial improvements Frederick made to the two-story cottage was a side addition to be used as a workshop. The side entrance for the cottage led from this workshop to the outside yard. But the principal portion of the house was equally as pleasing to the eye. A huge farmer's porch wrapped around the front of the cottage, offsetting the second-story bedroom, framed by a gambrel roof. A massive brick fireplace adorned one of the walls of the living room, and served as a focal point. In the heart of the kitchen was a recently acquired cast iron stove, which served not only for cooking, but for giving the room a warm, cozy feeling, even on the stormiest of days.

Seemingly, the only drawback to the cottage was its basement floor, which was constructed of fieldstone and often allowed water to seep into the cellar. Frederick Small had called Mark Winkley over to inspect the basement, to see whether there was anything he could do to make the cellar watertight. Mark Winkley was noted for his work as a mason, and suggested the only way to completely stop the seepage of water was to lay a cement floor. Frederick considered this option, but after hearing the cost of the project, felt that it wasn't worth the money. Thus, the Smalls put up with the annual spring flooding of the cellar, and the occasional foot or two of water that would fill the basement after a substantial summer's rain.

The calm and warmth of this Indian summer day was even more appreciated by all in Ossipee because the day before, they had experienced one of the heaviest rains ever witnessed in the town of Ossipee. The local people called them linestorms, which were made up of torrential downpours and strong winds, enough to topple old trees with weak branches and to fill most of the cellars in the area. Even with all the refurbishing Frederick performed on his lakeside cottage, the Smalls' residence was not excluded from this fate.

One would presume that with such a sensational storm, all the residents of Ossipee would bond together and support each other in the clean-up effort. But this assumption would only be considered possible by a person ignorant of the fractured nature of existence within the Ossipee region. For generations, Ossipee had been settled primarily by the families of woodsmen and farmers. However, in the mid-to-late 1800s, Ossipee became somewhat industrialized with the construction of sawmills and gristmills, powered by water wheels dipped into the generous supply of rapidly moving rivers flowing through the area. This sort of expansion was understandable, for it allowed Ossipee to become more self-sufficient in cutting its own lumber and grinding its own grains and corns. With the boom of the timber industry and the advent of more jobs, Ossipee's population grew, and a second neighborhood within the region of Ossipee was created called Center Ossipee. The economy flourished and optimism grew even stronger with the anticipation of a railway expansion to Ossipee, connecting its industries with previously out-of-reach markets. This created a desire for the mills to diversify by making more specialized products, and soon Ossipee was producing sashes, doors, blinds, shingles, furniture, and barrel hoops, among other products. A couple of mills even ventured into the tannery and textile industries. However, no one had predicted the actual effect the expansion of the railroad would have on the booming town of Ossipee. When the railroad arrived, it served to open area markets for competitors whose products were less expensive to produce. Although Ossipee's industries responded by creating even more specialized products, they couldn't compete in the expanded market. This had a devastating effect on the Ossipee region.

By 1900, the population of Ossipee had decreased significantly, dropping to about one-third of the population recorded in 1850. With the increased use of steam engines, mills were free to develop closer to the natural resources they relied on. Thus their dependency on riverside locations for power decreased dramatically. Many Ossipee residents, especially the younger generation, left to find work in the mills of Massachusetts, or to seek other positions in southern New Hampshire. This sudden decline in Ossipee's economy, bringing with it the abrupt loss of population, served to leave the remaining residents of Ossipee with a distasteful feeling towards outsiders, which developed into an adversary relationship between the native Ossipee residents and the seasonal residents and newcomers living out by the lake on the outskirts of Center Ossipee.

Although the town of Ossipee was further away from the lake than Center Ossipee, it held a distinction of its own within Carroll County, thanks to its 1839 representative to Concord, Asa Beacham. What saved Ossipee from anonymity was the coupe that Asa Beacham and his constituents were able to pull off in securing the sight for the Carroll County Courthouse in their sleepy little town. Many towns were vying for the courthouse, but it was Beacham who had the presence of mind to ask his constituents for donations for the building of the courthouse. At the close of business on Friday evening, Asa rode all night from Concord to Ossipee in a fierce attempt to return to Concord in time for the Monday morning vote. During his time in Ossipee, Asa collected contributions from several Ossipee residents, allowing Beacham to return to the legislators with a paper promising $850 toward the building of the Carroll County Courthouse in the town of Ossipee. Thus, it was decided and in April, 1840, a courthouse resembling a New England meetinghouse opened in Ossipee. Not only did it attract law offices to the town of Ossipee, but it provided substantial business to the nearby Carroll Inn, which was an old coach house diagonally across the street from the courthouse. To the left of the courthouse was the Charles H. Carter store, a general store which boasted selling, among other things, Quaker Oats. Two doors down stood the funeral parlor, and the blacksmith shop, a necessity in that day, even though motor vehicles were beginning to be more common in these parts of New Hampshire. The schoolhouse was about four doors down from the blacksmith shop; and across the street, the local church stood about two doors down from Brown's Store. That is, until 1915, when a terrible fire broke out in the town of Ossipee. The fire couldn't be contained, and the town lost its blacksmith shop, Carter's store, the funeral parlor, and worst of all, the Carroll County Courthouse. Rebuilding began immediately, since Ossipee didn't wish to lose its most prized acquisition. By December,1916, Ossipee once again had built its courthouse, this time a solid, more fire-resistant brick building, with huge white pillars in the front.

The second business district in the Ossipee region, Center Ossipee, was right around the corner from Lake Ossipee. Center Ossipee's most notable focal point was the beautiful Mountainview train station with its elegant gingerbread style trim. This railway station was Ossipee's link to Boston, as well as to other major cities in New Hampshire, such as Manchester and Concord, the state's capital. Across the street from the railway station stood the Central House, which served as an inn for Center Ossipee. This sprawling three-story inn had a large, circular tower with a farmer's porch wrapping around its front and a portion of its side. Another notable structure contributing to Center Ossipee's ambiance was Chamberlain's store, with Chamberlain Hall occupying the space above the emporium. This hall became more important than most had imagined, since while the courthouse was being rebuilt, Chamberlain Hall served as the site for court proceedings.

George Woodbury notes the relationship between the seasonal visitors and the Ossipee natives in his 1993 article that states: "Ossipee and the surrounding mountain country was not as used to summer visitors in 1916 as it is today. There was still a hard core of native-born farmers and woodsmen who viewed outsiders with suspicion. These were 'hicks' according to the summer residents who were themselves referred to locally as 'city fellers.' The distrust between native and outlander was marked."[1] However, the truth was that neither group could function well without the other, as the outsiders boosted the otherwise stagnant Ossipee economy, and the locals provided these newcomers with supplies, and occasionally, with transportation.

It was precisely 11 A.M. as Charles Sceggel, the grocer in Ossipee, marched up the steps of the Smalls' cottage to make a delivery. The Smalls had ordered a number of items including eggs, potatoes, soap, yeast, a broom, and five gallons of kerosene. Because very few families of Ossipee owned their own car, many people relied on Charles Sceggel's grocery delivery service. If they needed a ride somewhere, residents could call the day clerk of the Central House, George Kennett, who owned a spirited mare and a comfortable buggy that served as the taxi service in town.

Carrying the Smalls' packages up the steps of the farmer's porch from his truck was an effortless job for Charles, who was recognized as one of the most striking men in town. He was plenty strong, yet not muscle bound, with a white beard that came to a point, and one matching streak of white running through the top of his hair. He set the packages down on the floor of the porch, and gently knocked on the front door with his free hand as he leaned the broom against the wall.

Florence Small peaked out from behind a curtain and shyly smiled, allowing Charles only a glimpse of her large, yet somewhat sad, brown eyes as she looked down to open the door. Florence's curly, dark brown hair had been parted slightly off-center, and pulled back into a bun. Charles barely noticed Florence's slender, yet shapely figure, since it was somewhat hidden by the dark, full-skirted house dress she wore tightly buttoned around her neck. With groceries in hand, Charles brushed by Florence, making his way to the kitchen. As he unloaded the groceries, Charles spoke to Florence briefly, just making small talk to pass the time. Yesterday's linestorm, contrasting with the remarkably wonderful weather of the day, was a likely topic discussed that morning.

"Would you like the groceries on the shelf, like usual, Florence?" asked Charles in a friendly tone of voice.

"Oh thank you, that will be just fine," replied Florence, as she smiled shyly, turning to place the broom in a closet next to the kitchen. Florence always seemed to enjoy Charles' visits since she seldom saw many people at her isolated lakefront cottage, and Charles welcomed the chance to run groceries over to the Smalls' cottage whenever he had a spare minute or two.

"Nasty storm we had yesterday . . . . raining buckets for a while there. How'd you weather the storm out here on the lake?" Charles asked.

"Oh, we can't complain," answered Florence, as she placed the bar of soap by the kitchen sink.

"Well, today makes up for it though, don't it?"

Florence nodded with a grin, "Sure does."

"Where'd you like me to put the kerosene, Florence?" Charles asked, after unpacking the last of the groceries.

"In the can just outside the door would be fine, thanks," Florence answered.

Charles lifted the container of kerosene out of his truck and carted it up the steps. He carefully poured the kerosene into the large can near the front door.

"Well, I'll be seeing you. If you need anything more, just give a holler," Charles called from the porch, while checking to see that the kerosene was placed out of the heavy traffic areas.

Charles walked down the stairs and climbed into his truck, giving a casual wave back toward the cottage as he drove down the rutty dirt road towards town. In making this routine delivery to the Smalls' residence, Charles had no idea that he was about to gain the distinction of being the last known person to see Florence Arlene Curry Small alive.

The beautiful Indian summer day passed seemingly without incident, and no one was enjoying the day more than Edwin C. Connor, principal of the Alba High School. That is, until he received a phone call from Frederick Small. Ed had become affiliated with Small by participating in several joint insurance sales for which Frederick had initiated contacts. Although Frederick wasn't the type of person with whom Ed would normally choose to socialize, Ed had to admit that Frederick did have some good insurance contacts which were useful. And with the meager salary his job paid, Ed needed a second income in order to make ends meet. Frederick had advised him in many a venture that had proven profitable. Therefore, Ed tolerated Frederick's many vices, which included drinking to excess and using vulgar language even when ladies were in attendance, in the interest of continuing to receive this valuable information.

Frederick called Ed at his office that day to extend an invitation for Ed to join him on a business trip to Boston later that afternoon. Ed was a little annoyed at this sudden change of schedule, because this trip had previously been planned for the first week in October. This trip was to be unique because it not only included making contacts with prospective clients in Boston, but provided a chance for Ed to meet with a few possible insurance customers in the Manchester area as well. By changing the timing of the trip, the opportunity to break into the insurance market in Manchester would be placed in jeopardy, or at the very least, would have to be postponed.

"Ed, I've reserved two seats on the 4:07 train to Boston this afternoon for us, and booked a room at Young's Hotel for this evening. I thought we could take in dinner and a show tonight, and we could still make it back for Friday morning's school day." Frederick seemed to have thought of everything, but Ed hesitated.

"Frederick, it sounds great but I don't think I can get away today. The school day is underway, and . . . . I just don't see how I can make it. Why don't you take Florence instead? I'm sure she would enjoy a night out on the town. Besides, we're going away on that business trip next week. We can meet with potential customers then, and I was really looking forward to branching out and making some sales contacts in the Manchester area, too. Let's wait and do it all next week. The timing just isn't right, Fred." Ed tried to let Small down as easily as he could.

"Ed, I'd love to go next week, but something came up and I'm not going to be able to go out of town the first week in October. If you want to sell some insurance this month, this is the only time I'll be free to leave," Frederick retorted with an urgency in his voice. "Besides, the school day ends at 2:30. You'll have plenty of time to pack and get to the station."

"Well," Ed deliberated, " . . . . you're sure there's no other time you can go?"

"Sorry, this is the only day I can get away. And the weather's cooperating," Small assured Ed. "So I'll see you at the train station at 3:30 sharp."

"I'll do the best I can, but I can't guarantee," warned Ed.

"I'll be waiting for you," Frederick insisted, and hung up the phone, leaving Ed little chance of backing out. As soon as Frederick hung up the phone from arranging things with Ed, he quickly called George Kennett to arrange a taxi to pick him up at his cottage at about 3:15 P.M.

Now unlike Charles Sceggel, who visited the Smalls' home solely for the purpose of delivering groceries, George Kennett looked forward to the opportunity to stop by for reasons other than simply to provide taxi service. It seems that Frederick Small not only enjoyed his liquor, but was generous with it when he found somebody who was willing to drink with him, and perhaps share a story or two. Frederick would always invite George in for a little "nip"[2] or "snifter"[3] as they often called it, before embarking on any trip. George was greatly anticipating this snifter as he drove up to the cottage, and actually made an effort to arrive a little early, allowing time for a bit of socializing before the trip to the train station. Much to his disappointment, however, as George drove his mare up to the front of the cottage, he saw that Frederick was already waiting for him by the side door with his suitcase in hand. As George handed Frederick his mail from town, Frederick made no invitation for George to go into the cottage for a nip. Instead, Frederick opened the side door and placed the mail on a nearby table. Then, as he closed the door he called, "Good-bye, dear,"[4] and quickly limped toward the buggy where George stood waiting for him. Frederick was dressed in his best dark suit, accented with a fine, white shirt and a freshly starched collar, which was somewhat of a contrast to George's attire, which was more comfortably casual.

"Well, George, I'm glad you got here early,"[5] Frederick greeted George with a smile.

"Nice weather we're having this afternoon. What a difference a day makes," George responded, trying to conceal his disappointment. He lifted Frederick's suitcase into the back seat of his buggy, and held the carriage door open for him.

"You're right about that," said the short, graying Mr. Small as he stepped into the horse-drawn vehicle. After fastening the door for Frederick, George slid into the driver's seat and clucked to his young mare who proceeded down the road, head high and eyes wide. George carefully maneuvered the carriage down the muddy camp road towards the train station, avoiding the puddles leftover from yesterday's rains as best he could. Several times, he had to draw back the reins, when his spirited mare would break into a canter, resulting in a rough ride for his passenger. Frederick may have wondered why George put up with such an unruly horse, but it was well known that this spirited young mare was George's pride and joy. Besides, to the young mare's credit, the storm had rearranged the landscape of the area to a certain degree, and George's mare may have been leery of the occasional downed tree limb near the road.

As he drove up to the tracks, George saw Ed Connor standing by the curb near the train station, and Frederick directed George to drop him off with Ed. George was prepared to carry Frederick's bag to the train as he often had in the past. It was difficult for Frederick to carry anything heavy and still maintain his balance with his disfigured, undersized leg. But Ed insisted he could handle both Frederick's bag and his own.

"Besides, if you take the bag and wait for the train with us, your mare may become more unsettled," Ed maintained, noting the mare's fidgety, restless stance.

"Oh, she's got fire, but she's a patient girl just the same. She wouldn't mind me giving you a hand," George claimed as he stroked his mare on her neck, speaking calmly in an effort to reassure his horse. "But if you two are all set, I'll be heading back. Got some paperwork to finish up before Frank comes in to take over for the night."

Frederick and Ed bid George good-bye and shortly thereafter, the train steamed down the tracks, stopping close to where they had left their bags. The conductor helped Frederick up the stairs and as the train lurched forward, Frederick stumbled into a nearby window seat, leaving Ed with the seat on the aisle. The train was fairly empty and the two men enjoyed their ride to Boston. Upon arrival, Small and Connor went straight to Young's Hotel. After registering, Ed reached for their bags, only to be stopped by the bellhop who offered to bring the suitcases to their room for them. While settling into their lodging, Frederick called room service and ordered a bottle of rye to be delivered to their chamber that evening. Then both men left for the Parker House, a very prestigious restaurant in the heart of Boston, where they ate an elegant meal and talked over some future business plans. Following dinner, both men bought postcards for their wives. Frederick quickly composed the following note to his wife:

"Fair weather at Young's. Fred. September 28, 1916, 8:40 P.M."[6]

Frederick nudged Ed on the arm and giggled nervously as he showed Ed the postcard and told him, "Mrs. Small and I are always exact in all things."[7]

Ed smiled and after purchasing two stamps, Small and Connor were on their way to the Majestic Theater to see the new and somewhat controversial movie, "Where are My Children?" Following the movie, Ed and Frederick headed down Washington Street to Clarke's Grill, where they consumed a large portion of scallops and beer. The two men returned very late to Young's Hotel, and Ed groaned as he realized he had to get up early to catch a train back to Ossipee.

As they staggered toward the elevator in the hotel lobby, a clerk quietly called to the two men, "Are either one of you men a . . . . Mr. Frederick Small?"

"Yes, that's me," Frederick turned around to face the clerk.

"There was an urgent message that came in from the town of Ossipee, New Hampshire, earlier this evening, sir. They asked that you might call this number as soon as you returned tonight," said the clerk in a very sympathetic voice. The night operator had told the clerk of some very distressing information regarding Frederick Small, but the clerk chose to let Small find out for himself.

Frederick smiled at the clerk, then looking somewhat puzzled at Ed, stepped into a phone booth to make the call.

After what seemed like seconds, Ed, who had approached the phone booth at Fred's request, heard a thump. Ed swung around to find that Frederick had dropped the receiver and was leaning against the wall of the booth, sobbing uncontrollably.

"My God, it can't be true!"[8] Fred cried out.

"What's the matter, Fred? What can't be true?"[9] Ed couldn't imagine what had happened, and Frederick momentarily appeared to be incapable of speaking.

"You talk . . . ."[10] Fred managed to utter, as he motioned Ed to pick up the phone. As Ed stumbled into the phone booth, he faintly heard the voice of his old friend Frank Ferrin, the night clerk at the Central House in Center Ossipee.

As Ed put the phone to his ear he heard Frank trying to get a response from Fred.

"Mr. Small . . . . Mr. Small?" Frank questioned, "Mr. Small, are you still there?"

"Hello?" Ed interjected.

"Ed . . . . is that you?" Frank questioned. George Kennett had mentioned to Frank in passing that he saw Frederick meet Ed at the train station earlier that afternoon. George had assumed Ed was accompanying Frederick to Boston, as they often had done in the past. Frank was relieved to hear a familiar voice and the conversation that followed was as sensational as a small town hotel clerk could imagine.

"Frank?" Ed recognized the clerk's voice instantly. "Frank, what's happened?"

"About 10:00 tonight, all hell broke loose here, Ed. The fire horn blew, and as soon as I stepped outside, I saw where the fire was at. The whole Center village was lit up by the flames and sparks from the blaze. It was the Small place, out at the lake. You should have seen it, Ed! Soon as everybody in town looked out their windows, they cranked up their cars and headed out to the lake. Most of the folks from the cottages in the area were already at the fire . . . you know, neighbors hollered over to neighbors to let them know whose place was going up in smoke. But ya know, t'wasn't like any house fire I've ever seen. There was a column of smoke, but the flames and sparks were launched way up over the burning cottage, lighting up the whole damn sky as if it were daytime. Hottest damn fire I've ever felt, too. It was something to see!"

"This is unbelievable," Ed said, as he slouched back against the phone booth from the shock of the news. "Is Florence all right?"

"The first people on the scene were neighbors from a few of the surrounding cottages," Frank continued. "They called for Frederick and Florence, but nobody answered. There's no way anyone could have survived that fire anyway. By the time the fire department got there, the cottage was too far gone. It was impossible for anyone to get inside the cottage to search for Fred or Florence, although a couple of men tried the hatchway door. But the door was locked, or jammed, or something. They still aren't able to get inside to search the building. The firemen and volunteers have worked for hours hosing down the ruins, but the fire was so hot and the house burned to the ground so darned fast, it'll be a while before they'll be able to get in there. I heard a lot of local people remarking that it was almost as though the house had melted!"

"There's no sign of Mrs. Small?" asked Ed, not wishing to give up hope she had gotten out in time.

"No, they haven't found anybody yet," Frank answered. "We were all hoping the Smalls had been away for the evening, and when somebody at the fire mentioned they thought they saw you and Fred take the 4:07 to Boston, some folks ran down to your house to see if it was true. That's how we knew where to find

Fred. We hoped Florence had gone to stay with a friend for the night. A bunch of people took it upon themselves to run around town looking for Florence, but they never found her. Besides, if she was local, she'd have been down here watching the fire like everyone else was. But judging from Fred's reaction, I would say that as far as he knows, Florence was at home."

By now, Frederick was moaning, "I'm all alone in the world. I've lost my pet, my home, ... all gone. It can't be true!"[11]

"Was there an animal trapped in that fire, too?" asked Frank, who had overheard what Fred had said.

"No," Ed replied sadly, "that's Frederick's nickname for his wife . . . . his little pet."

"Oh," Frank hesitated, thinking a moment, "then Fred believes Florence was home all evening."

"Apparently," said Ed with a sigh, "We'll head home for Ossipee right away. It shouldn't take more than three hours or so to get there by car. Will you still be on duty when we get there?"

"I'll wait for you to arrive," Frank offered.

"Thanks. We'll see you then. Good-bye." Ed hung up the phone and requested that the clerk arrange for a car to pick them up and drive them back to Ossipee. There were no trains running at that time of night, and Ed felt it imperative that Frederick return home to search for his wife immediately. Ed was still hoping that after Frederick had left for Boston, Florence may have gotten together with a friend who insisted she spend the night with her. If she was out of town, Florence may not have even heard about the fire yet.

"My poor little pet,"[12] Frederick babbled as he paced the floor of his hotel room, while the bellboy and Ed quickly packed his belongings. "She must have sat too close to the fire while working on her needlework. I've always told her she sits too close to the fireplace, but she insists she needs the light to see what she's doing. An ember must have jumped from the fire to her nightclothes. My poor little pet. My poor, poor little pet. If only I had been there. My poor little pet." Frederick continued this pitiful whining all the way to the car.

The ride home seemed endless for Ed. Frederick would alternate his mournful whining, with relentless sobbing, and the phrase, "my poor little pet," while he guzzled the rye whiskey he had taken from his hotel room. It was about 4:30 A.M. when their car pulled up to the Central House in Center Ossipee. As Ed ran in to check if there had been any new developments in the story while they were en route, Frederick entered the dining room and ordered breakfast for the two of them.

Ed was surprised that Frederick could eat at a time like this, and suggested, "The car is waiting. I thought you'd like to go directly to see whatever remains of your cottage, Frederick."

"No, I can't bare to look at the old place on an empty stomach. It'll keep until I finish my breakfast," Frederick grumbled, and exhausted, Ed sat down to watch Frederick eat a considerably large, country-style breakfast.

As it turned out, Small and Connor were two of the few people remaining in Center Ossipee. Most of the townspeople were out at the lake gawking at the disaster, or volunteering to help the sheriff search the ruins for clues to the origin of the fire, and the whereabouts of Mrs. Small. But the search didn't look like it was going to be productive. All that appeared to be left of the cottage was the blackened fieldstone foundation, which had once supported Frederick and Florence Smalls' home.

[1] George Woodbury, "Ossipee Recalls: A Murder That Was Too Perfect," *Home Town History*, April 22, 1993, pg. 1.

[2] Frank C. McLean, "Florence Small Slain In the 'Arson Engine Perfect Crime'", *The American*, Feb. 21, 1936, pg. 4.

[3] Ibid., pg. 4.

[4] Ibid., pg. 1.

[5] "State Arrays Its Evidence Against Small," *The Manchester Union*, Oct. 6, 1916, pg. 2.

[6] McLean, pg. 2.

[7] Ibid., pg. 2.

[8] Ibid., pg. 2.

[9] Ibid., pg. 2.

[10] Ibid., pg. 2.

[11] Ibid., pg. 2.

[12] Ibid., pg. 2.

III. The Murder

It was just about 6:30 A.M. when Frederick Small arrived at the scene of his smoldering cottage. Ed Connor and Frank Ferrin, who had just gotten off work at the Central House, accompanied Frederick to the site. As the men stepped from the car, they were immediately met by the smell of smoldering wood. Both Frank and Ed marveled that the building had been completely leveled by the fire, without any of the framework of the cottage still erect. The only part that remained of the Small cottage was the towering brick chimney. The charred area surrounding the cottage made the chimney appear statuesque, standing steeple-like in the early morning sun.

Small, Ferrin, and Connor were by no means solitary figures examining the tragic scene. It seemed a few of the locals became suspicious of the fire as they watched it burn and decided a call to the sheriff, Arthur Chandler in North Conway, was in order. Chandler's jurisdiction included the entire Carroll County area. Thus it was his duty to head an investigation when foul play was suspected. Chandler, who was described by some as being as big as the region he represented, arrived at the scene with his deputies before Frederick Small had returned from Boston, ordering spectators not to touch anything and to stand back from the debris. The sheriff anxiously awaited Small's arrival, while volunteers began digging in the ash and rubble, examining the scene for any clues of how the fire may have started. The hope that Mrs. Small was away from the cottage at the time of the fire had all but vanished, since she still had not been located. Thus the grizzly task of locating the remains of Florence Small fell to Chandler's team of investigators.

Frederick just shook his head in disbelief as he stared at what used to be his home, then wandered over to the volunteers, who were meticulously digging in the smoldering remains, having been warned they were looking for anything that wasn't totally consumed in last night's inferno. Frederick watched for a moment, then called to the men, "There is $6,000 worth of jewelry there and anyone who finds it can keep it. I am through with it."[1] The sheriff watched as Small made his way to where the entrance to the cellarway had once stood. As Small tried to enter the cellar, Chandler was there to stop him, giving the likely explanation that this was the sight of an ongoing investigation, and the burned out structure could not be trusted to be safe. With that, Small somberly turned and limped back to the car, asking Frank to take him to the Central House where he would need to reserve a room for an indefinite period of time. Ed helped Frederick back into the car, informing Small of his intentions to remain at the scene and help out however he could. Frank approached the front hood to crank the engine until it turned over, rattling its passenger. Then Frank slid into the driver's seat, and slowly drove down the road, back toward Center Ossipee. Chandler and his deputies studied the car and its occupants as it rolled out the driveway and down the wooded, dirt road.

While relaxing in the sitting room of the Central House, Small reiterated his theory, on many occasions, as to how he thought the fire may have gotten started. Frederick would begin by saying, "It was customary for my little pet to sit by the fireplace while working on her sewing. She did such fine needlework, you know. But on more than one occasion, I've brushed away a glowing ember that jumped from the fireplace to her nightclothes when the fire crackled. If I had only been there last night, it all may have been prevented. If I'd only been there. My poor little pet! I've lost everything now . . . . gone in the ashes." Then Frederick would stare at a corner of the room and sigh a deep, heavy, mournful sigh.

Back at the lakeside lot, the sheriff was interviewing many of the firefighters and spectators who had witnessed the tragic blaze. There were three things that especially puzzled firefighters, as well as many of the bystanders, while the blaze burned out of control the night before. First, the flames were hotter than any fire they had ever fought. The coolness of the air had little effect on the intense heat that was emitted from the fire. It was almost as though the fire was being fueled by something other than the wood of which the home was constructed. Secondly, the building burned so swiftly that many of the Smalls' neighbors who saw the cottage when flames were first visible, stated the cottage ignited in a manner that was just short of an explosion. The funnel of flames and sparks that rose high above the framework of the cottage penetrated the night sky with a vast illumination of everything around it, which could be seen from miles away by residents of Center Ossipee. Finally, Frank had mentioned to Ed that the fire was most unusual to him because it appeared the entire building was burning evenly. Chandler knew that information obtained from eyewitness accounts often proved helpful, and he tried to keep these observations in mind while searching through the rubble of the old cottage.

A customary inspection of the grounds of the Small property and the neighboring cottages and docks revealed several unsettling discoveries. A boat that had been pulled up on shore for winter storage was found to have a hammer inside it, while another craft held a more intriguing towel with discernible blood stains on it. Because there were few cottages nearby still occupied at the time of the fire, since most of the seasonal crowd had moved back home by then, the owners of the property were unavailable for comment. Thus, the importance of these discoveries was unclear. Furthermore, a few witnesses who were perusing the area the night of the fire came forward to tell of footprints found in the sand down by one of the docked boats. It was unknown at the time whether any of these findings would have a bearing on the disappearance of Mrs. Small, but Chandler took note of them just the same.

As Chandler returned to the cottage ruins, a deputy approached with one of the first eyewitnesses to arrive on the scene of last night's blaze. "Thought ya might be interested in what this man has to say. He was lookin' in the window last night when the fire first started, to see if the Smalls were still inside." The deputy introduced one of the Smalls' neighbors, Elmer Loring, to his boss.

The witness shook hands with the sheriff, then began to express his concerns for Mrs. Small's welfare. "Course I couldn't get too close to the building, the fire was burning so hot, but I was able to see what looked like a woman about the size of Mrs. Small. I tried to get in for a closer look, but the flames were all around her by then."

"No chance of getting in there to pull her out?" Chandler asked.

"I tried the hatchway door, but it was locked or jammed or something . . . . I couldn't get in," Loring answered. "But here's the peculiar part. I ran back to the window to see if I could tell if she was still alive; but after a real good look, I swear the burning object that I thought was a woman's body appeared to have been tied to the bedpost. So I ran to try the door one more time, and when I came back to the window, the bed and the woman were gone. Now I know that sounds crazy, but it's what I saw."

The sheriff thought for a moment, scratching his chin, then shook the man's hand. "Well, thanks for coming forward. If you think of anything else you saw, let me know."

"Will do," Loring answered, then added, "I don't mean to be pointing a finger at anybody, but things just didn't seem right to me is all."

"Just another piece in the puzzle," Chandler answered thoughtfully. "Put all the pieces together, we may just have a crime here."

The painstaking task of digging through the remains seemed endless, as well as fruitless, because every piece of debris that was found appeared to be burned beyond recognition, and the searchers were beginning to lose hope they would ever find the answer to what happened to Florence Small. But when volunteers had cleared a path to the cellar, expectations were raised. As they made their way to the basement floor, officials saw what appeared to be debris from the upper levels of the house, jutting out from a foot or two of pooled water, held in by the fieldstone cellar walls. Chandler was elated by the news, and volunteers were soon wading knee deep in murky, tepid water for clues. Amazingly, some of the contents of the cottage had not burned. In fact, many items had fallen through the floor into the once cool water in the cellar, which had saved them from the flames that had consumed the rest of the cottage.

Nobody relished the thought of wading through this stagnant pool of water collected in the cellar. But many items were compiled that were considered significant to the investigation.

Items were meticulously recorded and marked by Dr. Hodsdon, a retired medical examiner from the area who participated in the search, before being turned over to the sheriff and his men. One of the most surreal discoveries found by the base of the chimney was the kitchen sink, partially leaning on a black cast iron stove, which appeared to still contain the unwashed crockery from a meal which Mrs. Small apparently hadn't managed to clean up before her disappearance. Curiously, a section of the top of the stove had been melted in the fire, and a strange, crusty material was found close to the melted section. A bedspring could be seen leaning close to the stove, and considering the eyewitness's previous report, this was of special interest to Chandler.

On the way to that corner of the basement, Ed Connor and others recovered a spark plug, a clock spring, a fire screen, an alarm clock, and some hairpins; all to be tagged and removed, although their significance was not clear. As they arrived at the corner of the room where the bedspring and a portion of a mattress lay, Connor rotated the bedding, enabling him to pass it along to the cellarway where it could be removed. However neither Chandler nor Dr. Hodsdon, nor the volunteers, nor especially Ed Connor, were prepared for what they were about to witness. With the rotation of a portion of the bedpost and the partially scorched mattress, the half-burned, smoldering torso of Mrs. Small appeared, her head preserved by the pool of water that had sheltered it from the flames. Connor splashed water on the smoldering torso, then gingerly carried the body to Dr. Hodsdon, who was waiting near the cellarway at the other end of the basement.

Chandler aided Dr. Hodsdon in the retrieval of the body, bringing it into the sunlight for a closer look. Dr. Hodsdon was intrigued to find two layers of cloth wrapped around Florence's head. Upon closer examination, Hodsdon found that the cloth had been bound in place by a partially burned rope that was twice strung around Mrs. Small's neck, then neatly tied in a square knot at the base of her skull. The flesh on the front of her body had been burned beyond recognition. However, the internal organs and the basic skeletal structure of the body remained intact. Even the back of Mrs. Small's garments had remained virtually untouched by flames. Unfortunately, Florence's arms and legs had been completely consumed by the inferno, and would provide no additional clues to add to the investigation. Mrs. Small's body was carefully removed from the site and taken to Dr. Hodsdon's barn for further examination.

Feeling that he finally had concrete evidence of a crime, Chandler placed a call to County Solicitor Walter E. Hill in Newburyport, Massachusetts, where he was conducting business. Hill returned to Ossipee by car at once, but wasn't expected on the scene until first thing the next morning. Chandler also called Attorney General James P. Tuttle in Manchester, to recruit him into the investigation. These two men would have the primary responsibility of building a case if it became necessary to prosecute the crime.

While Ed Connor was taking a much needed break, feeling the necessity for a bit of fresh air, he caught a glimpse of Small's boat-house out of the corner of his eye. Visualizing the cord wrapped around Florence's throat for a moment, he flashed back to a point in time when he and his wife had accompanied Fred and Florence Small on an afternoon boat trip. Frederick Small had rigged a cord to connect the lever on his boat to the steering mechanism, for ease in manipulating the boat in the water. That afternoon, however, the steering mechanism had become jammed. Connor remembered this cord in such detail because he was the one who released the obstruction and freed up the steering apparatus. Ed couldn't shake the feeling that this cord bore a striking resemblance to the cord he had just seen tied around Florence Small's neck. Feeling a sudden, cold, shudder as he began to realize the implications if the cord belonged to Frederick Small, Ed Connor strode over to the boathouse. Much to Connor's horror, the cord had been removed from Frederick Small's boat. Connor leaned against the boathouse, shrinking to the floor to sit for a moment, trying to figure out the meaning of this discovery. Could it be that he had spent the former evening with a man who had just killed his wife and set his home on fire? Had he been duped into providing Small with an alibi by agreeing to accompany Frederick on this last-minute excursion to Boston? How could this be true? How could Small have acted so natural? For a man to carry off such a deed, and truly act so nonchalant, he would have to be some kind of monster! Besides, anybody could have gained access to the Small's boathouse and stolen the cord. For that matter, the rope from the boat could have been stored somewhere else and the similarity of the ropes may have been a coincidence.

Chandler interrupted Ed's train of thought, when he approached to see if Ed had found anything in the boathouse.

"It's not so much what I found, but what I didn't find that's so bothersome," Ed answered, and continued to explain about his disturbing discovery.

Meanwhile one of the sheriff's volunteers, Frederick Bean, was finding further evidence in the basement. In his quest, Bean managed to find most of Mrs. Small's jewelry, including a ring with two modest stones in it, a diamond band, a wedding ring, and a watch. This jewelry didn't begin to reach the dollar value given by Frederick Small when he addressed the volunteers earlier that morning. And some folks thought it odd that jewelry was the first thing to come to mind when Small was initially faced with the image of his burned cottage, and the uncertain fate of his missing wife.

Searchers also found a .32 caliber revolver in the cellar waters. It was recovered while sifting through the rubble close to a portion of the Smalls' bed, which had fallen from the bedroom above. Strangely, a small section of the metal bed frame and bed spring had melted in the fire. In the same area, some men's undergarments were found rolled tightly into a small ball, with the strong scent of kerosene radiating from the whole bundle. All of these items were found relatively close to where Florence's body had been recovered.

Outside the cottage, several volunteers and a couple of newspapermen were searching the grounds on the west side, near where Small had left his cottage for the final time. They were looking for any trace of evidence that would suggest what had happened the night before. In the course of the morning, several men handled a lock, which was thought to have been from the side door of the cottage. Arthur Brunt had held the lock in his hand, noting the key inside the lock and the bolt out, suggesting the door had been locked at the time of the fire. However, no one knew who picked the lock up first or how many times the key had been turned. Brunt threw the lock back to the ground, feeling it of little significance to the investigation. Newspaperman John Casey was the last man to pick up the lock before handing it over to the sheriff, who saw the key turned twice in his presence. Thus, by the time this evidence had been recorded and tagged, no one could be absolutely certain whether it was originally found in the locked position, or whether it was unlocked at the time of the fire.

When John Casey and another reporter, Roy Atkinson, returned to the cellar, they saw Dr. Bartley Carleton, a local garage keeper, locate some pieces of German silver wire in the middle of the cellar, along with a bundle of telephone wire. In addition, volunteers happened upon some blood stained bedding, corset hoops, and a poker. All these remains were bagged and tagged, and investigators felt lucky to have salvaged so much from this destructive inferno. But the greatest loss of all, of course, was the life of Florence Arlene Curry Small, not yet forty years old.

It was Dr. Horne's duty as chief medical examiner from nearby Conway to call the Central House and notify Frederick Small of the discovery of his wife's body.

When Dr. Horne asked, "What shall we do with the body, Mr. Small?"[2] Frederick demonstrated notable amazement.

"What, is there enough left of the body for a casket?"[3] he responded.

Dr. Horne explained to Small that, indeed, a significant portion of his wife's body had been preserved by the pool of water in his basement. After momentary consideration, Small made the decision to buy a $35 casket and a half burial lot in the town of Ossipee. Dr. Horne promised to make the arrangements for Frederick, then proceeded to Dr. Hodsdon's barn to perform a preliminary autopsy on Florence Small. Upon completion of the autopsy, it was arranged for Florence's body to be stored in a vault in Ossipee, awaiting burial.

Shortly after the body of Mrs. Small was sent to Dr. Hodsdon's barn, the sheriff, feeling certain that he was faced with a murder rather than an accident, went to the Central House to confront Frederick Small with his findings. Small was distraught with the news and immediately offered $1,000 reward to anyone who was able to disclose information that would lead to the arrest of his wife's killer. Small personally was of the opinion that a tramp was responsible for the crime, and was quite adamant in stating his belief publicly. This was not an unusual conclusion in the early

1900s, since tramps were considered so menacing that in 1878 the state legislature of New Hampshire actually passed a Tramp Act to discourage unemployed vagrants from wandering through its regions. Residents of New Hampshire considered "the new image of the tramp to be sinister: tramps were associated with violence, they were considered to be labor agitators, and they were held up as a bad example to others because they were supposedly lazy and immoral. The very fact that tramps were homeless was threatening in an era when domesticity meant respectability." [4] Tramps had been seen in most towns in New England from time to time, and although a few of the vagrants were local men down on their luck, nobody really knew the background of many of the transient vagrants. It was certainly possible that a tramp could have broken into the isolated cottage, thinking it was off-season and the cottage was probably unoccupied. While searching for food or valuables, a tramp could have been confronted by Mrs. Small, and a struggle might have ensued. The tramp could have used anything found in the home to challenge Mrs. Small, and the struggle could have turned ugly. A fresh load of kerosene had been delivered to the cottage that morning, which could have served to fuel a fire and conceal the crime.

It wasn't much later that day, however, that Chandler took it upon himself to place Frederick Small under protective custody in the Central House, pending orders from Walter Hill. From this point on, Frederick Small no longer spoke freely about the events of this incident, his theories about the fire or killer, or even his life in general. Instead, Frederick Small called an attorney, Sidney Stevens of Somersworth, who publicly stated, "it doesn't seem possible that Mr. Small could have murdered his wife." [5] Shortly thereafter, William Matthews, also of Somersworth, was retained as co-council for the defense. It was well known in the Ossipee area that Matthews' former senior partner, James Edgerly, had previously represented a man named Joseph Buzzell, who was the defendant in an earlier case that included capital punishment as a choice of verdict. Joseph Buzzell was, notably, the only Carroll County resident, to date, who had ever been convicted of his crime and hanged.

That evening, Chandler told a reporter from *The Manchester Union Leader* that a preliminary autopsy showed evidence that Mrs.

Small's skull had been crushed by a blow or blows to the head with a blunt instrument such as an ax or a hammer. In addition, a clothesline had been twisted firmly around Florence's neck and tied in a knot at the back of her head. Chandler also noted an additional wound to Mrs. Small's head which bore resemblance to a gunshot wound. These wounds weren't initially evident at the time of the discovery of the body, since Mrs. Small's face was concealed by a piece of the bedclothes, or possibly underwear. A more conclusive autopsy was to be performed over the weekend, when representatives from both sides of the case could be present. Chandler's intent was to reassure the residents of Ossipee by announcing that Frederick Small had been taken into custody for the murder of his wife. The idea of a random killer at large in the vicinity of Ossipee would have been very unsettling to the residents.

The following day, two doctors arrived in Ossipee from Somerville, Massachusetts, to represent the interests of Frederick Small at the official autopsy. It was found that Florence Small had initially suffered a gunshot wound to the left side of her forehead. The wound measured six inches deep and one-half inch wide, and the bullet exited into Florence's right jaw, shattering her jawbone. The bullet was recovered from Mrs. Small's skull, and was found to match the caliber of revolver found in the ruins of the cottage.

It was also found that although the bullet wound had the potential to kill Mrs. Small, she was further beaten about the head several times with a blunt instrument, possibly a fireplace poker. Furthermore, Florence's scalp had been opened up in three places by what is speculated to have been a coal slicer. These wounds were not thought to have been fatal.

Remarkably enough, the assailant wasn't finished. Doctors theorized that perhaps Florence may still have been crying out. To silence her finally, the attacker took a cord and tied it twice around her throat, so tightly that Mrs. Small's tongue protruded from her mouth. Then the cord was tied in a perfect square knot at the base of her skull. The intent of the cloth mask covering Florence's face was still a mystery, since no hint of chloroform was found, which might have been administered in this manner. However, there was strong evidence that a sticky, organic substance called resin, which burns with a smoky flame and a pungent odor, had been rubbed all over Florence's body. Resin was thought to have been used by the murderer in an effort to completely destroy any trace of Mrs. Small's corpse. Had it taken longer to recover Mrs. Small's body, the remains could very well have been destroyed, since resin is insoluble in water. This would explain why Florence's body was discovered burning slowly, long after the cottage fire had been extinguished.

Medical authorities made the decision to sever the head of Florence Small from the rest of her body, being careful to cut below the point where the cord was still bound around her neck and throat. This was to be preserved as evidence in case a trial were to be held. Florence's stomach was placed in a jar to be brought to Dartmouth College by Dr. Horne for further examination of its contents, in hopes that he could pinpoint the time of death. A segment of Mrs. Small's intestines was also collected, which contained a significant amount of melted resin. Although the front of Mrs. Small's torso had been burned severely, her back was only discolored by the fire, leaving much important evidence still intact. This was a lucky break for the forensic team.

A coroner's inquest was held on October 2, 1916, revealing the cause of death as strangulation. The inquest began with medical evidence from the autopsy, which was reported by Dr. Hodsdon. Following the medical testimony, Frederick Bean testified that he had found a revolver and Mrs. Small's jewelry in the basement of the cottage. Dr. Hodsdon subsequently added that the caliber of bullet removed from Florence's right jawbone matched the revolver found by Frederick Bean in the cottage ruins.

When the attorney general asked the sheriff if Frederick Small had made any remark at all about his wife's death, Sheriff Chandler stated that Small insisted his wife was alive when he left for the station. Chandler reiterated Small's claim that he said good-bye to his wife as he left the cottage in George Kennett's carriage, and Small maintained that George Kennett could back up his story, since George witnessed his departure from his home. However, after questioning George Kennett earlier that day, the sheriff relayed George's recollection of the event by stating that although George did recollect Frederick calling good-bye as he left the cottage, George didn't remember seeing or hearing Florence answer. Chandler also reported that the fire was discovered at approximately 10:10 on the evening of September 28, and by 11:30, the cottage was completely consumed by flames.

Judge Charles S. Miles presided over the district court session that immediately followed the coroner's inquest. Frederick Small's lawyers entered a plea of not guilty for their client. The reading of the warrant was waived, and court was adjourned until October 5. At this time, Frederick Small was remanded into custody and taken to the Ossipee jail.

Florence Small's remains were transported to a local tomb in Ossipee. Arrangements had been made for a service to be held on October 3, however burial could not take place until after the October 5 hearing, or until the whole matter had come to a conclusion. Florence's corpse had become one of the key pieces of evidence in the circumstantial case against her husband. A Reverend Small, no relation to the defendant, was commissioned to perform the funeral ceremony, and a burial plot, which had earlier been purchased by Frederick at a local cemetery, was readied for his wife.

With Frederick Small safely locked away in the Ossipee jailhouse, some boys from the surrounding area were drawn to the Small cottage ruins in search of adventure and possibly some undetected treasure. It was well known that a full $6,000 worth of diamonds and jewels had yet to be found, and there was talk by some of the townsfolk that the jewels were still there, in the ruins of the cottage. The local guide in town, Frederick Bean, who had been so instrumental in finding much of the evidence in the ruins of the cellar of the Smalls' cottage, felt it his duty to guard the cottage from potential looters and vandals. Bean spent several nights on watch at the ruins, during which time some strange, inexplicable occurrences took place. On more than one occasion, Fred Bean noticed a peculiar light flash about 100 feet from his position. Furthermore, at various intervals of his stay, Bean believed he heard footsteps. Although local investigators took Bean's claims seriously, they were never able to explain these peculiar incidents. Were they a product of an overactive imagination, the result of tenacious treasure hunters, or the effect of some extraordinary phenomenon? Although Fred Bean would later testify about these occurrences at the hearing on October 5, he had to wonder what conclusions officials from the Boston area would draw concerning him and his interest in the property he was guarding, which aside from the fieldstone foundation, lay in destruction.

[1] "State Arrays Its Evidence Against Small," *The Manchester Union*, Oct. 6, 1916, pg. 2.

[2] McLean, pg. 3.

[3] Ibid., pg. 3.

[4] Timothy Dodge, *Crime and Punishment in New Hampshire, 1812-1914*, Volume 1 (Durham, NH: University of New Hampshire Dissertation), 1992, pg. 232.

[5] "Small to Face Charge of Murder in First Degree," *The Manchester Union*, Sept. 30, 1916, pg. 1.

IV. CIRCUMSTANCES

As headlines throughout the country reported the invasion of Rumanians into Bulgaria, the small village of Ossipee had more important business on its mind. With no witnesses to Florence Small's murder, and with her husband, Frederick, having an airtight alibi, placing him several hundred miles away in Boston on the evening of Florence's projected time of death, the circumstantial case against Small had to be built with the utmost of care. Upon the advice of lawyers, Frederick Small remained completely mute to any questions advanced by investigators, enduring in silence what he considered to be his unjust incarceration, while waiting to be exonerated from this crime. However, even as Small was restrained from actively participating in the investigation, fortune seekers searching in the ruins of his cottage for unrecovered jewels turned up new pieces of evidence, the most significant of which was a bullet cartridge that apparently had been missed during the initial search. The empty shell matched the size of the Colt automatic pistol found in the rubble close to Mrs. Small's body. This new piece of evidence was welcomed by the sheriff and the prosecution team, who had assumed that all the valuable exhibits had been recovered. The prosecution's investigators had shifted focus from the ruins to actively attempting to trace any recent purchase of a substantial quantity of resin, which had covered the body of Mrs. Small. Because resin was commonly used by boaters to seal and waterproof their vessels, a receipt from this purchase wasn't considered a necessity, since resin could already have been stored at the Small residence.

Yet if evidence could be located of a recent, sizable purchase of resin by Frederick Small, it could prove convincing to a jury.

Later on that morning of October 3, a modest service was held for Florence Arlene Curry Small in the Congregational Church in Center Ossipee. A single, floral wreath adorned the coffin. This solitary, floral offering was sent by Florence's husband, Frederick, displaying a ribbon marked with the word, "Love."[1] Florence's mother, Elizabeth Curry, and her sister, Norma Curry, attended the service officiated by the pastor of the church, Reverend Small. The Currys had made the trip from their home in Somerville, Massachusetts, specifically for the purpose of attending Florence's funeral. Nevertheless, when the service had ended, James Tuttle, attorney for the prosecution, approached the two women, interested in setting up an interview while they were in New Hampshire. Tuttle hoped to learn something about Frederick's marriage to Florence which would be helpful in prosecuting his case. However, he found his efforts to be in vain, for the Currys were far too upset to be interrogated at that time. Tuttle traveled as far as Manchester with the two women, then granted them some privacy in their return home to Somerville. But he hoped to make an appointment with the Currys for some time in the near future to resume their conversation.

As the day of the hearing approached, public speculation grew. It was determined that the hearing would be held in Chamberlain Hall, which when not being used as a makeshift courthouse, served as the community's dance hall. There couldn't have been worse timing for a high-profile case such as this, since the town of Ossipee was reeling from the fire that had destroyed so many of its public and private facilities. It must have been somewhat embarrassing to have to perform a critical autopsy, with out-of-state officials present, in the barn of the town's retired medical examiner, when the pristine conditions of a funeral home or a medical examiner's office would have been more appropriate. In addition, although the construction of the new courthouse was on schedule, its projected opening was not until December 1916.

To add to the less than impeccable conditions in the town of Ossipee, rumors among the townspeople were surfacing as well. One of the most disturbing rumors concerned Mrs. Small's stomach, and other samples of her organs. Rumor had it that while Medical Referee Frank Horne was en route to Dartmouth College with a suitcase containing Mrs. Small's remains, he and his suitcase had become parted at Boston's North Station and Mrs. Small's organs had disappeared. However, this rumor was later dispelled as a misinterpreted phone conversation. According to Dr. Horne, he had never gone to Boston, and Professor H. W. Kingsford at Dartmouth College had already identified the substance on Mrs. Small's intestines to have been resin.

One of the most interesting pieces of evidence that Chandler was readying for the prosecution was a compilation of articles Frederick Small brought with him in a satchel on his trip to Boston. A search of this satchel gave investigators much to ponder, since some of the items included could lead one to believe Small had previous knowledge that his home and all its contents would be destroyed while he was away. The first articles Chandler pulled from the satchel were the obvious belongings that most men of the era would have taken with them on an overnight—a couple of handkerchiefs, a hair brush and comb, two shirts and a black bow tie, a shaving brush, some soap, three razors, a pair of barber clippers, and a toothbrush.

Reaching in a little further, Chandler unpacked a box of Rexall salve, a bottle of dental toothache gum, and a nickel catheter—articles that must have made the sheriff wonder about Mr. Small's health, yet these items weren't incriminating.

As the sheriff dug deeper into Frederick Small's satchel, the items got more interesting as well as suspect. It was natural to have a fountain pen filler, especially when planning to conduct business, but a Masonic lamb-skin apron? What possible purpose could Small have had for this in Boston? Such an item, inscribed with the words: "F. L. Small, Portland Lodge, No. 1, Maine, Saturday, March 13, 1889,"[2] must have been an invaluable keepsake to Small.

As he held the soft apron in his hands, Sheriff Chandler had to have been asking himself, "Why would Frederick Small take a keepsake like this with him on an overnight business trip to Boston? Unless, of course, he knew he was going to lose it in a fire."

The satchel had become far more than a routine cataloguing of items for the prosecution; it became a new and intriguing piece of evidence for the sheriff. As Chandler continued to empty the satchel, he came across two letters written by the same person, whose signature was somewhat illegible. One was dated December 14, 1908, and the other April 20, 1909, both signed by a person who appeared to have been named "Lama."[3] Still more intriguing, underneath the letters, the sheriff found the warranty deed to the Small's cottage, inscribed "A. L. Hodsdon and wife to Emma S. Harton-Carroll County Records, Ossipee, Received July 17, 1914."[4] Any one of these belongings included in Small's satchel might not have been suspicious, but for Small to have carried so many important, and in most cases, sentimental items with him, Chandler conceded Small must have known these items would have been lost forever if he didn't take them out of his home before he left for Boston.

The most intriguing of all articles packed in the satchel, however, appeared to have been handwritten on three pages of Parker House stationery while Small was in Boston. Unfolding the stationery, Chandler read the list entitled, "Inventory of Home and Shop."[5] The items on the list were arranged by room, and a column to the right of each item reflected their values.

Scanning the list, Chandler noted the total value of possessions equaling $3,429.60. Then turning to the last page, Chandler found another $309 of belongings, leaving a total of $3,738.60 in assets, which must have been destroyed in the fire, if Small's list was accurate. And one would have every reason to believe the list was meticulously executed, for not only did it include furniture and knickknacks, but the final two items listed fourteen Cuban cigars and twenty-five pieces of hard peppermint candy in a candy dish. Small was impeccably precise, and from all appearances he seemed to be safeguarding his chances that his insurance would reimburse him for every single item in the cottage, no matter how minute. The curious point was, why would Small include such disposable items as candy and cigars in his inventory, unless he knew precisely what the number was going to be at the time of the destruction of his property? Unless, of course, Small was using the average number of cigars and candy he customarily kept in these dishes. But why would he be writing down that kind of information at all? For that matter, why would he take old letters, a Masonic apron, and the deed to his house on an overnight trip to Boston, unless he didn't expect them to be there when he returned home the next day? And there was more—a couple of diaries (1910 - 1914), and an address book—all taken to Boston with Small the afternoon before a fire.

Considering the effort Frederick Small made in including every minute possession in his inventory, there were two articles conspicuously missing from the list. Small neglected to itemize any of the $6,000 worth of jewels he so generously offered volunteers who were digging in the cottage ruins. The search for these valuables proved fruitless in the end, since only a few modest pieces of jewelry were ever found. This led many local people to wonder if the jewels had ever existed from the start. Also absent from the inventory was the revolver recovered from the ruins, just a short distance from Florence Small's body. This item certainly held more value than the pieces of peppermint candy detailed in the list, and it was a huge oversight that the article was not included. Unless, of course, Small knew this weapon was used in the crime and was willing to take a loss on its value in an effort to keep from calling attention to its existence.

When specifically asked about the items found in his satchel, Small reasoned that he was bringing them to Boston to open a safe deposit box at one of the local banks. The two letters signed by a woman whose name appeared to be Lama, were actually written by Small's second wife, Laura, who he had divorced several years earlier. Small's account of his behavior was logical. However, if Small wasn't responsible for the murder of his wife, he had to have been one of the luckiest men on earth to have decided to remove his sentimental valuables hours before his cottage was consumed in flames. Or conversely, perhaps he was the most unlucky man on earth, considering these items couldn't help but draw increased suspicion his way.

On the morning of October 5, both the prosecution and the defense stood ready to reveal their cases. The morning was dry, with only a touch of chill in the air, as Frederick Small walked across the street to Chamberlain Hall, in the company of Fred Bean, Deputy Sheriff George Philbrick, and a group of curious townspeople, reporters, and spectators from the surrounding countryside. Most of the men were dressed in suitcoats, although Fred Bean wore only a pair of dress pants and a short-sleeved white shirt. Frederick Small was notably shorter than most men attending the hearing, crossing the street with a significant limp as he tried to keep pace with the others. Small's knee-length dress coat was incongruous with the rest of the men's attire, and contributed to his slight appearance. Both sides of the street were lined with cars and carriages, giving more the impression of a convening Sunday service rather than a court hearing getting underway. The one notable exception, however, was the absence of many women at the proceedings.

Of all the evidence presented in the case, most notable was that which the prosecution failed to furnish. Results of the analysis of Florence Small's organs, including her stomach contents, were not yet available, thus eliminating the prosecution's ability to determine Florence Small's approximate time of death, leaving the door open for the defense to argue there was really no testimony provided that could eliminate the possibility that Mrs. Small was, in fact, alive at the time of Frederick Small's departure from the house.

Although Frederick Small had consistently felt that George Kennett's testimony could prove beneficial to his case, it proved to be far more damaging than either man had wished, due to the inferences made from George's lack of ability to back up Frederick's claim. In answer to the prosecution's question concerning seeing or hearing a response by Florence Small to her husband's farewell, George Kennett had to admit that he recollected no sign of Mrs. Small's presence. George told the court, "Small turned and said 'Good-bye,' apparently to Mrs. Small, but I did not see her, nor did I see any waving of hands or anything else to indicate her presence in the house."[6] However, George qualified his statement with the remark that he hadn't paid too much attention to Frederick Small's departure from the cottage since he was distracted by his high spirited, young horse. Thus, George's testimony was not proof that Florence was dead at the time of her husband's departure, although many perceived this to be true, due to George's inability to collaborate Frederick's story that Florence said good-bye to him when he left for the train station. George always enjoyed Frederick Small, and was notably uncomfortable in his role of witness for the prosecution. But as unpleasant as these proceedings were for George, he felt an obligation to honestly answer the questions put to him, and was relieved when his testimony was complete.

Ed Connor, who unlike George Kennett appeared to have little difficulty testifying against his former business associate, perhaps harboring feelings of betrayal, feeling that Small may have duped him into providing an alibi for this horrendous crime, told members of the hearing that the cord wrapped around Florence's throat particularly resembled a cord Small had rigged in his motor boat. Mrs. Connor took the stand as well, verifying the cord's similarity to that which she saw in Frederick's boat. Next Frank Ferrin took the stand to verify details of the phone call placed to Small in Boston the night of the fire. Then Dr. Horne and Dr. Hodsdon presented medical testimony, with Dr. Horne noting the presence of a substantial amount of resin on Mrs. Small's body. Dr. Hodsdon furthered Dr. Horne's testimony by volunteering that "the use of resin might tend to make destruction of the body complete, but the process would be a slow one."[7]

Information revealed for the first time at the hearing finally gave authorities, as well as puzzled locals, a possible motive for Small to have committed this heinous crime against his wife. Winfield Chase, a rural delivery carrier from the neighboring town of Wakefield who also sold insurance on the side, took the stand and told of two insurance policies he had drawn up for Frederick Small, insuring his cottage for the amount of $3,000 and his possessions for $1,000. Charles A. White was called to the stand next. He was the man who sold the cottage to Frederick Small in July 1914. When asked by the prosecution to inform the court of the price the defendant had paid for his cottage, White's answer was ordered inadmissible by Judge Miles, ruling on a motion from the defense. However, anyone who was familiar with the Smalls' property, with its prime location and panoramic views on the shore of Lake Ossipee, knew that with all its attributes, its value didn't begin to approach the sum of $3,000.

To add further to the issue of motive, Ed Connor took the stand once again to attest to the fact that Frederick Small had called him in February of that year to have a joint life insurance policy drawn up for his wife and himself. After several meetings, the policy was finally accepted for the amount of $20,000, payable to the survivor in the event that one of the Smalls outlived the other, with Frederick's nephew being the sole beneficiary if both the Smalls were to die concurrently.

Small's disclosure at the scene of the ruins whereby he publicly stated, "There is $6,000 worth of jewelry there and anyone who finds it can keep it. I am through with it,"[8] was brought forth by the prosecution through the testimony of Ed Connor. With the introduction of this statement, the prosecution hoped to indicate Small's intent to interfere with the investigation, since he had to have known this would attract fortune hunters to the scene of the crime. Also, by claiming there were valuables that were not subsequently recovered in the ruins, the prosecution concluded Small was cunningly attempting to establish theft as a motive for the murder of his wife.

With this final testimony, the hearing was adjourned until October 6, at which time the state was to resume with closing arguments, and Frederick Small's defense team would have an opportunity to begin its case. Subsequently, a new autopsy was ordered for Mrs. Small's body. Florence's remains were, once again, taken from the vault and carried back to Dr. Hodsdon's garage, where a medical examiner from Boston, Dr. George B. Magrath, performed the third autopsy. This postmortem lasted into the night, at which time Florence was returned to her casket and her interim tomb. Although there was no official reason given for this third autopsy, rumor had it that the authorities were having difficulty establishing the fact that Florence was dead at the time Frederick left his house to catch the 4:07 train. The prosecution was hoping to determine that Florence was not attacked before she was shot, strangled, and torched. Proof of an attack only served to solidify Small's explanation, leaving authorities with no other recourse than to ignore the defense's explanation that this crime was committed after Frederick left the house.

Chamberlain Hall was packed the following day, when the decision of whether Frederick Small would be ordered held for grand jury would be made. As it turned out, it didn't take long for this judgment to be reached. Apparently James P. Tuttle's summation was persuasive. "This man had the motive, he had the apparent means, he is such a man as would commit the crime. He is the man who did commit this crime."[9] Judge Miles ordered Small to be held for the grand jury. This decision was made prior to the defense being given an opportunity to present its case, even with the significant defect in the prosecution's case whereby they could not establish whether Florence was dead or alive at the time of Frederick's departure.

A petition was immediately entered by the defense for a change in venue. Especially after these proceedings, the defense was adamant in declaring that the local people who make up the total registered population of Carroll County were prejudiced against their client. The defense urged the court to hold Small's trial in Strafford County, which was not too far from Ossipee, and would minimize the traveling expenses and fees witnesses would be subject to pay with the change in venue. Strafford County was toward the coast, southeast of Carroll County and included the cities of Durham and Dover (the county seat of Strafford). Surely this slight increase in cost would be worth the certainty that Frederick Small would receive a fair and unbiased jury. The defense felt this a reasonable request.

The attorneys for Frederick Small then proceeded with their defense strategy. Although they offered no witnesses at this time (it had been speculated that six people would be called to testify in Small's defense), William Matthews argued the injustice of holding his client for trial, and even offered a possible alternative suspect for the crime. The certainty the defense held in its theory that this crime had been committed by a person searching for liquor, resulted in the spotlight resting upon Fred Bean, the local guide who so generously volunteered to search in the rubble for evidence and to guard the Small property following the fire. Matthews pursued this theory by addressing the court with the words, "What do you think of the evidence of a man who does not remember his whereabouts on that day (Sept. 28, 1916) or night, and who did not know how he received the scratch on his face? I do not accuse Mr. Bean of the crime, but it might be used as a parallel case."[10] Further persevering with his theme that a local man was responsible, Matthews added, "The hearing held here offered the court an opportunity to search out the real criminal and bring him to justice."[11] Apparently there was good cause to suspect Fred Bean of this crime, for he admitted he had been drinking heavily on the day of the crime, and indeed had blacked out on the day of September 28. Furthermore, Fred Bean couldn't remember anything from the night of September 28.

Matthews further charged that the people of Ossipee would have thought ill of Mr. Small if he hadn't performed his duty as head of the household to secure a life insurance policy to provide for his family in the event of a death. "That was only reasonable protection,"[12] Matthews proclaimed. Matthews furthered Small's cause by arguing that Frederick Small was in the public eye from the moment he left his cottage for Boston until the hearing, and all who saw Small agreed concurrently that he behaved as any normal man would, "unmarred from any unnatural act. His feeling was one of real grief."[13] In summation, counsel for the defense stated, "Mr. Small is a man of honor and intelligence. No man of intelligence would have bought kerosene oil at 11 o'clock in the morning for the purpose of firing his home."[14]

Attorney General Tuttle countered these remarks by Matthews with the final statement of the hearing. The theory that was broadly accepted by the prosecution, the defense, and the general public was that the person who torched the dwelling must have been the same person who murdered Florence Small, since the purpose for the fire appeared to be to conceal evidence of the crime. Tuttle urged the judge to consider the household inventory found in Small's satchel. To the prosecution, the composing and possession of this inventory was, in and of itself, evidence that Frederick Small had prior knowledge there was to have been a fire in his home. "If he knew there was going to be a fire," Attorney General Tuttle deduced, " he also knew there had been a murder."[15] Tuttle further speculated on how the fire was set when he surmised that a candle floating on a block of wood in a large quantity of kerosene could easily have sparked a flash fire of the kind that destroyed the Small cottage. He then disclosed the fact that the can of kerosene found in the ruins of the fire had been emptied.

Throughout the course of the hearing, Frederick Small's demeanor was one of stoicism. Although he was observed weeping at several points in the case, Small was generally composed for the duration of the hearing.

The arguments that Matthews presented on Frederick Small's behalf had little impact on Judge Miles' previous decision. Small was remanded into the custody of the sheriff's department once more. George Philbrick escorted Small from Chamberlain Hall to once again take up residency in the Ossipee jail while awaiting his appearance before the grand jury, which was scheduled to resume sessions in December. However, neither the prosecution nor the defense was able to fill in the gap of time between Small's departure to Boston and the discovery of the fire shortly after 10:00 P.M. There had been no evidence presented by either side to affirm whether Florence Small was dead or alive when George Kennett arrived to take his client to the Mountainview train station on the afternoon of September 28, 1916. The prosecution counted on the testimony of Professor H. W. Kingsford of Dartmouth College, who was analyzing the stomach contents of Mrs. Small. Perhaps Florence's charred torso held the only clue to her activities later that day. The defense, however, was following a different path, going back to the cottage ruins to examine the scorched door that had once secured the hatchway entrance to the cellar of the dwelling. If this hatchway was unlocked at the time of the murder and subsequent fire, it could have provided easy access for an intruder to enter and escape the cottage. The defense was also investigating the old-fashioned lock which was found near the side entrance of the cottage. If the side door was found to have been locked from the inside, as eyewitnesses to the fire maintained, Florence must have been alive when Frederick left for Boston to turn the key and lock the door.

It was often whispered locally that on the morning of September 29, when Frederick Small was examining what remained of his lakeside cottage, he was overheard mumbling about the water in the basement that had always proven bothersome to him. Local folks swear they distinctly heard Small say, "Look at the water in that cellar. Mark Winkley did that job and he is the cause of all my troubles."[16] This statement angered all who knew Mark Winkley, who was considered to have been one of the most skillful artisans in Carroll County. In the words of a farmer from Tamworth named Jim Welch, "Mark Winkley was one of the best stone-masons ever lived in these parts and his cellars and walls are his memorial on this earth." [17] Ironically, the once cursed water that seeped into the cellar of the cottage to entomb Florence

Small's body, may have aided in preserving the hatchway door of the cottage, which could prove to exonerate Frederick Small from this heinous crime of which he stood accused.

[1] "Empty Shell is Found in Ruins," *The Manchester Union*, Oct. 3, 1916, pg. 1.
[2] *Inventory of Articles Found by Sheriff Arthur W. Chandler in the Traveling Bag of Frederick L. Small at Mountainview, Ossipee*, Carroll County Courthouse, Sept. 29, 1916,   pg. 1. (Item 3)
[3] Ibid., pg. 1. (Item 21)
[4] Ibid., pg. 1. (Item 19)
[5] Ibid., pg. 1. (Item 20)
[6] "State Arrays Its Evidence Against Small," *The Manchester Union*, Oct. 6, 1916, pg. 2.
[7] Ibid., pg. 2.
[8] Ibid., pg. 2.
[9] "New Autopsy on Mrs. Small's Body," *The Manchester Union*, Oct. 7, 1916, pg. 1.
[10] Ibid., pg. 1.
[11] Ibid., pg. 1.
[12] Ibid., pg. 1.
[13] Ibid., pg. 1.
[14] Ibid., pg. 1.
[15] Ibid., pg. 1.
[16] Marjorie Gand Harkness and Lilian C. McGrew, *High Sheriff*. (Tamworth, NH: Tamworth Historical Society, 1960) pg. 92.
[17] Ibid., pg. 92.

V. DISCOVERIES

In the days immediately following Frederick Small's hearing, the Ossipee region was treated to clear, dry, comfortable weather with temperatures slightly higher than normal. Having had little opportunity to interview acquaintances of the Smalls prior to the hearing, the county solicitor, Walter Hill, and the attorney general, James Tuttle, took advantage of the favorable weather to get outside and talk with some local residents who had known the Smalls. Because of Frederick Small's ties to Boston, Massachusetts, and Portland, Maine, this trial was likely to draw regional scrutiny. The murder trial of Frederick Small was sure to sustain record attendance, including many reporters. Thus it was imperative in upholding the reputation of the state's attorney general's office that the prosecution achieve a conviction.

An individual who turned out to be influential in depicting a destructive image of Frederick Small's relationship with his wife, was Philip L. Davis, the Small family's milkman and mail carrier. The attorney general's office may first have noticed Mr. Davis when he found himself in possession of an undeliverable postcard, addressed to Florence Small. This postcard was sent by Frederick Small to his wife from Boston the evening of the fire. Considering what happened that night, the unnaturally precise words of Frederick Small gave authorities all the more reason to be suspect. "Fair weather at Young's. Fred. September 28, 1916, 8:40 P.M." [1] These carefully selected words must have had quite an impact on the prosecution team. The postcard was documented as evidence that Small had prior knowledge of the fire. The postcard's purpose seemed self-evident. What would the precise time the postcard was written matter to Florence? This was hardly typical postcard text. It served to provide nothing more than the time, date, weather, and location of the writer. There was no mention of yearning for Florence's company or of wishing she was there in Boston with her husband. And Frederick never remarked about his train ride to Boston or anticipated activities, even though he had quite a full evening planned with Ed. Why bother with silly details when the author knew the addressee was dead! Then again, perhaps Frederick Small considered his trips to Boston a "boys night out," and wasn't about to fill his wife in on the details of his evening away from home. This could very well have been the case, but why, then, would Frederick bother to write a postcard home at all? In reality, it must have appeared to investigators that Small wasn't truly writing the postcard to Florence, he was writing it to the Carroll County authorities. He was saying, "See, at this precise time, on exactly this day, I was in Boston. Whatever's about to happen in Ossipee, I had no hand in." It appeared that Small was trying every angle to make certain his alibi was firmly established.

Adding to the discovery of the postcard, authorities were further informed of incidents of alleged abuse observed by Philip Davis. It seemed that in the course of the last two and a half years, Davis was witness to a couple of unpleasant altercations between Florence and Frederick Small. The first incident was to have occurred while Mr. Davis was delivering mail to the Smalls. As Davis approached the Smalls' cottage, the couple was attempting to raise a flagpole on their property. The project was not going well and Frederick Small became angry and frustrated when the pole fell to the ground. Frederick apparently blamed Florence for the entire mishap, and Davis witnessed Small venting his frustration by kicking his wife, while swearing at her.

In a separate incident, Davis told Tuttle of a time when he had accompanied Frederick and his wife on a duck hunting trip in 1914. Although Philip offered to row the boat, Frederick insisted that Florence was quite capable of the task, since she came from sturdy stock. Unfortunately, in the course of the trip, Florence ran the boat aground on one of the many sandbars that plagued the river. She endeavored to push the boat clear of the bar, but her repeated efforts proved unsuccessful. Frederick became agitated and yanked one of the oars away from Florence. Having raised the oar over his wife's head, Frederick, from all indications, seemed poised to hit her. Davis immediately reached forward and grabbed the oar from Frederick's hands, preventing him from striking his wife. Frederick, then, turned to Davis and said with a smirk, "Do you think I'd hit her?"[2]

"He threatened to brain her with an oar,"[3] Attorney General Tuttle mumbled as he noted the event in his records.

Following his visit with Philip Davis, Tuttle spoke with a neighboring couple who lived in a cottage near the Smalls' home. They similarly painted a picture of Frederick as a domineering, abusive husband. Mr. and Mrs. George D. Emerson, who permanently resided in Quincy, Massachusetts, told the attorney general that while they were attending a card party at the Smalls' about five days before the fire, Florence accidentally misdealt the cards. Frederick became furious at his wife, and scolded her so harshly that Florence was reduced to tears. George's wife further stated that when they had returned to their cottage that evening, she heard a woman's piercing screams coming from the Smalls' home.

The attorney general continued to take down pertinent points from each incident, ". . . . another night after he had caused her to be weeping by his rough and ugly language a yell came from his cottage."[4] Tuttle discovered that it was common for occupants of the neighboring cabins on Lake Ossipee to hear screams originating from either the Small cottage or from their boat when they were trolling in the middle of the lake. This apparently occurred on a regular basis, and although folks were somewhat disturbed by the shrill screams, nobody thought much about it as a life threatening situation. Privately, most folks' sympathies rested with Florence. However in 1916, a man's home was his castle and what occurred in a private home was a private matter. As long as Florence continued to appear unscathed by these incidents and was happy enough to continue living in the same home with Frederick Small, what man or woman in the community would have taken it upon himself to break up the household, even though it had the appearance of some dysfunction? Furthermore, in 1916, it was difficult for abused women to leave their husbands, since work was hard to find, and it wasn't socially acceptable for a woman to leave a marriage. As the wedding vows said, a wife was expected to love, honor, and obey her husband, and if obedience was not adhered to, a man was expected by the community to keep his family in line.

While accounts of Small's temperamental character grew, other aspects of the case were being addressed as well. A gentleman who authorities were extremely interested in talking to was Charles E. Merritt of Manchester, who was a general agent for John Hancock Mutual Life Insurance Company in Boston. In February 1916, Frederick Small placed a call to Ed Connor to arrange for a joint life insurance policy to be drawn up for his wife and himself. Initially, Ed contacted Winfield Chase, who had previously issued a $3,000 fire insurance policy for Small's property and possessions. However, Chase informed Connor that he didn't handle life insurance policies. Instead, Ed was encouraged to refer Small to Charles Merritt, who subsequently drew up a policy payable to either survivor,—either Florence or Frederick; or in the event that both should die, the named beneficiary was to be Frederick Small's nephew, Nathaniel N. Mitchell.

Although a joint application was originally submitted by Frederick and Florence Small, as it turned out, two separate applications were needed to secure the policy. The necessity for this deviation from procedure arose because there was a problem with Florence's signature. In short, it wasn't hers. Frederick Small had signed Florence's name to the application, stating that as her husband, it was his right to do so. However, Merritt insisted that Frederick Small secure his wife's authentic signature on the document, and rejected the original joint application. Realizing there was no other means to acquire the insurance other than to have Florence sign it, Frederick did eventually produce his wife's genuine signature on the policy. Although Merritt, Connor, and Small had met at the cottage to cover the terms of the policy, Florence had never participated in the discussions, remaining in a separate room while the particulars of the policy were being drafted.

On March 13, 1916, Frederick paid the first annual premium on his policy. The total bill came to $1,107.60, which was a significant amount of money for most people in 1916. However, after studying Frederick Small's bank records, the prosecution team realized that this was an especially large sum of money for Frederick Small to pay for a policy year after year. When the next annual premium was due in March 1917, Frederick was going to have to pay roughly one fourth of his total savings to maintain this policy, taking into consideration that the balance in Frederick's savings account was $4,455.05. It appeared this policy was to become more and more of a liability every year that Frederick didn't collect on it. Barring some sudden influx of money, Frederick couldn't afford to carry the policy for much more than four additional years, assuming there was no unforeseen household or medical liability during that time period.

Although Ed Connor knew nothing of Frederick Small's financial status, he found one inquiry of Small's particularly troubling in light of the dubious information that had been surfacing since their trip to Boston. Small asked this question in the car on the way home to Ossipee the evening of the fire, at a time when he was alternately taking swigs of rye and sobbing for his poor little pet. Small glanced at Ed through swollen, bloodshot eyes and said, "Do you think there will be any problem with Merritt?"[5] At first, Ed didn't understand what Small meant, since he had been focusing on the tragedy. Then, Ed chalked it up to the man being beside himself with grief and worry for his wife and property. But when he realized Small was referring to the whole life insurance issue, Ed found it difficult to believe that Small had actually thought of insurance during a crisis such as this. However, who knows what strange courses one's mind takes when confronted with a life altering tragedy.

In light of what authorities perceived to be a strong motive for the crime—Small's recovery of insurance money for the loss of his property and death of his wife—it may have crossed their minds that the scheme to totally destroy Florence's body may not have been in Frederick's best interest in reaching this goal. Insurance companies often impose a waiting period on the beneficiary when a body can't be recovered as proof of death. With Small dabbling in the insurance industry himself, he must have been familiar with the rules concerning the payoff of life insurance claims. He had to have known that the payoff would be quicker and easier if a body had been recovered. It would seem to have been extremely careless for a man as meticulous as Frederick Small, to plan the total destruction of his wife's body if insurance money was his motive for killing his wife—if he killed his wife at all. However, John Hancock Mutual Life Insurance Company states that as long as there is a presumed death, where authorities confirm there was a fire and the woman was presumed to have been in the dwelling at the time of the fire, the insurance claim would have been paid off. One of the few cases when a policy claim would be held up for a court decree would be when a person simply disappears without a trace. Another instance would be when the beneficiary is somehow implicated in the disappearance or death of the insured individual.

When the paperwork concerning Florence Small's stomach analysis arrived in Ossipee from Dartmouth College, both the prosecution and the defense teams felt cause for jubilation, each feeling they had finally received significant evidence to prove their cases. Dr. Kingsford's report revealed that Mrs. Small's stomach contained pieces of red meat, vegetables, and cucumber seeds, which were virtually undigested. Although the time of death was somewhat difficult to pin down, the professor of pathology speculated that Mrs. Small died about a half to three quarters of an hour after eating this meal. Then, qualifying his statement, Dr. Kingsford summarized that Florence Small could not have died any more than an hour after eating. The prosecution immediately went to work attempting to establish the time of day the Smalls customarily ate dinner. Mrs. Lilla Ferrin, wife of Frank Ferrin, was quick to volunteer that the Smalls usually ate their heartiest meal at noontime. Ed Connor was able to collaborate Mrs. Ferrin's statement, as he too had always seen the Smalls eat their biggest meal in the middle of the day. With this new evidence, the prosecution finally had the information they needed to pinpoint the time of Florence's death. If she customarily ate her heartiest meal, which would ordinarily consist of meat and vegetables, at noontime, then she had to have been murdered in the early afternoon, shortly after finishing her meal. Since Frederick Small hadn't left for Boston until after 3:00 P.M., he had plenty of time to murder his wife, set up some kind of timed incendiary device, and make his way outside to wait for George Kennett to take him to the train.

Although the prosecution was certain they had all the information needed to establish a time of death that made it feasible for Frederick Small to have committed the crime, the defense was working with the same information, coming to a totally different conclusion. According to the defense, the fact that Florence's stomach contained undigested red meat and vegetables proved her husband didn't murder her, since her time of death had to have been far later than the prosecution had projected. According to Frederick Small, he and his wife had a light lunch of canned shrimp in the early afternoon. With her husband not coming home for supper that evening, the defense speculated that more than likely, Florence had warmed over some stew or soup at the supper hour, and upon completion of this meal, an intruder broke into her home and killed her. Both the prosecution's and the defense's solutions were feasible. However the defense's theory hinged on the word of Frederick Small, that he and his wife did, indeed, have shrimp for lunch the day she died. It would be up to the jury to decide if they could trust Small's account of what turned out to be his final meal with his wife.

The prosecution was becoming aware that most adults in the area had a tendency to avoid Frederick whenever possible. Small had an abrasive personality, which most people assumed was a result of his harboring inferior feelings concerning his disability; which in 1916 was more accurately referred to as a deformity. Because of his shorter, disfigured leg, Small never felt quite good enough, and attempted to cover his feelings of inadequacy with an annoying boastful manner. Although Small would occasionally help a neighbor with minor electrical work, most local people got the impression he spent his time alone with his wife, since he seldom participated in community events.

But when news of the murder of Florence Small hit the Boston papers, people began to speculate about the fate of Frederick Small. After reading about the murder in Ossipee, one Boston police inspector actually called the prosecution team, having formerly met Small during a court proceeding.

Inspector Andrew Houghton's interest in the case dated from 1914, when he attended a courtroom session in which Frederick Small was bringing suit against a Boston newspaper. During the trial, Small was overheard by Houghton telling his wife, "If you open your mouth I'll kill you."[6] Although Houghton was troubled by both Frederick's words and tone of voice, he never mentioned it to anyone. He attributed his lack of intervention to having no real reason to report the incident, since he didn't seriously consider this to be a genuine threat to Florence's life. However, the incident left a lasting negative impression of the character of Frederick Small. It wasn't until he found out the murdered woman was the same one he heard threatened in the courtroom that he decided to step forward.

Although this reference to Small's character was extremely relevant to the case, especially when taking into account that the report came from someone outside the Ossipee region, the prosecution still feared it could be regarded as suspect by the jury. After all, this was the first time Houghton had mentioned this matter after years had passed. If this incident had left such a lasting impression on the inspector, why didn't he tell someone about it when it first occurred? Perhaps Andrew Houghton held a grudge against Small for a totally unrelated reason, and saw his chance for payback in this case. When Houghton became aware of the prosecution's concerns, however, he quickly defended his assertion by referring the attorneys to Norma Curry, Florence's sister, who he claimed also overheard the abusive statement.

With this significant addition to their case, the prosecution felt it crucial to reconnect with the Curry family. Attorney General Tuttle wanted to respect the privacy of Florence's mother and sister in coping with their grief, but he felt the family's focus may have shifted from the loss of their loved one to desiring her death be avenged. To this end, Tuttle was searching for details that give background on Florence and Frederick's relationship prior to their arrival in Ossipee. It was highly possible that the Curry's might have recognized some foreshadowing of this tragedy, where a pattern of behavior or events might be established. Background information to which the Currys alone were privy may have held the key in predicting this family's misfortunes. Indications may have been apparent years previous to the couple ever coming to Ossipee, previous to the life altering tragedy which befell their beloved Florence in the isolated cottage, and previous to Frederick's fate being seemingly sealed by a leak in the old fieldstone foundation.

[1] McLean, pg. 2.

[2] "Small Had Made Threats," *Concord Evening Monitor*, Dec. 28, 1916, pg. 1.

[3] The State of New Hampshire Superior Court, *State vs. Frederick L. Small: Respondent's Bill of Exceptions*, Carroll County Courthouse, Dec. 1, 1916, pg. 22.

[4] Ibid., pg. 22.

[5] McLean, pg. 4.

[6] "Had Heavy Insurance," *Concord Evening Monitor*, Dec. 29, 1916, pg. 1.

VI. The Romance

As the skies grew gray and the air turned colder, Tuttle made a second attempt to contact the Curry family at their home in Somerville, Massachusetts. Located just slightly north of Boston, Somerville had easy access to Boston's North Station, which provided direct trains to the Ossipee area. Much to the relief of the attorney general, both women were anxious to provide any information that would help the prosecution's cause to convict the man they believed murdered Florence.

The meeting between the prosecution team and Norma and Elizabeth Curry took place shortly after the initial phone call, in an undisclosed location. Elizabeth Curry, Florence's mother, made a favorable impression on all who became acquainted with her in the Ossipee area. She was a calm, matronly, dignified woman who put people at ease. Although Tuttle had originally thought Elizabeth Curry to be a widow, he found that Florence's father was still alive. However Mr. Curry's health had been failing, forcing him to retire from his position as sea captain, which had afforded them a beautiful farm in Southborough, Massachusetts. By the time Florence Curry had met Frederick Small, her father's health had deteriorated so much that he was forced to move to a seamen's home in New York called Sailor's Snug Harbor. Thus, no effort was made by the prosecution to talk with Mr. Curry, since it was thought that he never met Frederick Small, and thus lacked any information concerning the man his daughter was to wed.

However, Elizabeth Curry and her daughter, Norma, were extremely helpful in providing facts concerning the courtship and marriage of Frederick and Florence Small. Florence had not lived her entire life in New England; she was born in Hortenville, Nova Scotia, and was well into her thirties when she met Frederick in Southborough. In 1916, it was common for a woman of thirty-two to be labeled a "spinster" or "old maid," and Florence and Norma were surely aware of their social standing. Florence was pleasing enough in appearance to have attracted many men. However, Southborough, Massachusetts, was a rural community, which didn't offer two young women living on a farm much to choose from in the line of suitors. Thus they took care of the farm and their mother while their father was away at sea, and when their father could no longer provide for the family, the Currys converted their farm into a convalescent home. This was the first opportunity the girls had to meet men from out of town. Many eligible men would come to visit their sick relatives, and initially Tuttle thought that Frederick was, perhaps, one of those men.

However, Frederick came to the farm for a different reason. With the two sisters and their mother involved in caring for patients and managing their home, they found they needed a handyman, who could take care of those things that a husband very often would handle around the average household. Without their father around, the farm was beginning to fall into disrepair. Thus, Mrs. Curry placed an advertisement in the Boston paper for a handyman to take care of normal maintenance around the home, and Frederick Small answered the ad. Small was very good at fixing things that were broken and even had some practical knowledge of electricity. He especially enjoyed working with telephone wiring.

Frederick Small appeared to be the perfect choice for handyman, and Florence and he quickly became friends. According to Mrs. Curry, Frederick loved to talk—about himself, his former marriages, and big investment deals. From what she heard, Mrs. Curry wasn't impressed. She found Frederick to be boastful and self-absorbed. But Florence was taken by Frederick and in fewer than six weeks, they were married. Mrs. Curry had to have wondered if Florence wouldn't have been taken by virtually any man she hired to work in the house. Although it is certain that Florence's mother would have tried to convince her daughter to wait until she knew the man better, Florence had her mind set on marrying Frederick.

The newly married couple appeared to be happy at first. Then Norma got word that the nurse at their convalescent home had summoned Doctor Bacon on Florence's behalf. Apparently Florence had gone to the nurse for medical advice in treating a wound to her head. Upon initial examination, the nurse felt the cut too severe to handle herself, and thus Dr. Bacon, the family physician, was called.

Dr. Bacon frequently visited the convalescent home to treat patients living there, and was comfortable opening the door and walking in. Upon walking into the kitchen, he found Florence sitting in a chair, her face covered with blood. When Frederick saw Dr. Bacon he sprang to his feet yelling, "Who the hell called you? What are you here for?"[1] Then, according to what Dr. Bacon told the Currys, Frederick picked up a piece of wood from a box that was stored by the stove and charged at him, ready to do bodily harm. But he was no match for the size and stature of Dr. Bacon. Dr. Bacon picked up one of the chairs from the kitchen set and raised it in the air. As Frederick approached, Dr. Bacon swung the chair, sending Frederick Small sailing across the kitchen. One of Frederick's legs slid under the stove and became lodged there. When Dr. Bacon saw that Small was going nowhere, he approached Florence to begin treatment. When he asked her what had happened, Frederick bellowed, "God damn her, I hit her on the head with a boot jack. I'd ought to have killed her, and I will yet!"[2] Dr. Bacon was appalled at Frederick's behavior, but there wasn't much he could do about it, except to dress Florence's wounds and report the incident to the police. This was the first indication the Currys had of an abusive side of Frederick Small.

Shortly after this incident, Frederick announced that Florence and he were moving to New Hampshire. The Currys were not happy about the move. With Florence nearby, they could keep an eye on the household to guard against further cases of abuse. Because Florence was married now, she either had to follow her husband or leave him, and Florence choose to follow him. Any objections the Currys made fell on deaf ears, and they had to watch helplessly as Florence, who had lived in the Curry household for the past thirty-two years, departed their home with her husband, headed for the Ossipee region of New Hampshire.

What happened next was as much of a surprise to the prosecution when they discovered it as it was to the Currys when it occurred. When Florence and Frederick were about to be married, Frederick had papers drawn up to provide for a division of the Curry property, to assure that Florence would receive her rightful share of an inheritance in the event of a death in the family or some tragedy befalling the property. Once Florence's share of the property had been identified, Frederick insured Florence's share for ten thousand dollars. Coincidentally, the day after Florence and Frederick moved out of the Curry's Southborough homestead, heading for their newly acquired cottage in New Hampshire, a fire of unknown origin leveled the Curry farm. All the dwellings that made up Florence's inheritance had been completely destroyed. At the time, nobody thought much about the fire. There were no fatalities, and in 1914, house fires were fairly common. But in light of the recent incident in Ossipee, the Currys must have wondered whether their own misfortune had somehow been caused by Small. As handyman, he had access to all their buildings and could easily have made something unsafe in the old farm, which had the potential to destroy the facility. Or perhaps through the accidental burning of the Curry farm, Small realized how easy it was to be awarded insurance money through some unforeseen event. The destruction of the Currys' farm may actually have been a coincidence, and Small may have had no hand in the incident whatsoever. Regardless, having been forced to leave Southborough by the devastating inferno, as they were unable to rebuild, the Curry's took what few belongings they were able to salvage and moved to the city of Somerville. In sharp contrast, Frederick Small collected a fast $10,000 on the insurance policy, keeping the money for himself.

Having been satisfied in knowing the details concerning Frederick and Florence's brief courtship and marriage, the interview turned to earlier times in Frederick Small's life. It was well known by all in Ossipee that Frederick had been twice married, prior to his marriage with Florence. The *Manchester Union* newspaper provided a brief summary of the Smalls' family history shortly after the fire. However, because of Frederick's strong urge to talk about himself, the Currys knew details about Small's life that were not common knowledge.

When he first arrived at the Curry home, Frederick often spoke of his youth and his former marriages. In 1890, when he had just turned twenty-one years old, Frederick secured a job in a small grocery store just outside of Portland, Maine, his hometown. It was there that he met and eventually married a woman named Nettie Davis, who resided in Minot, Maine. Frederick was married to Nettie for about a year and they were awaiting the birth of their first child, when tragically, both Nettie and their baby died in childbirth. This had to have been a devastating blow to Frederick Small, who even in his youth, never seemed to get a break in life.

Frederick seemed to have been star-crossed at an early age, when his dreams of being a professional baseball player were shattered by a serious injury to his leg. In his youth, Frederick Small was a budding star athlete, who was more adept at playing baseball than any of the other boys in the Portland area. As a star on his high school baseball team, Frederick must have enjoyed all of the prestige associated with such stature. However, tragedy struck one afternoon as Frederick Small slid into first base, colliding with another player. His leg was broken in several places, and doctors were unable to set his leg so it would heal normally. One leg remained significantly shorter than the other. This life-altering injury served as a devastating blow to Small, denying him his perceived destiny of greatness. This injury, coupled with the loss of his first wife and child, must have served as a bitter reminder of how unfair the world had been to Frederick to this point.

But Small rebounded from these experiences by moving around, trying his hand at many different kinds of jobs, with none really to his liking. Frederick eventually moved to Boston, where he brokered stocks. In time, Frederick met his second wife, Laura M. Patterson, from Salem, Massachusetts. They were married in Everett on July 31, 1899, and moved to Brigham Farm in Hudson, until it was destroyed by fire in 1900. The couple then moved to Boston, and finally to Somerville, where they lived in a house on Rogers Avenue. Neighbors report that Frederick and Laura appeared very much in love with each other, but didn't mix with others in the neighborhood very often. Laura was described as a very quiet, serene woman, who had a tendency to be extremely shy. She often sat alone in a rocking chair on the front porch of her Somerville home, where she rocked endlessly. Neighbors who knew the Smalls were surprised when in 1908, Frederick brought suit for five hundred thousand dollars against a man named A. H. Soden, charging him with alienation of his wife's affections. The *New York Times* noted this to be the highest amount of money ever sought for damages in a suit of this kind in the United States. Soden was a distinguished sportsman who had once been part owner of the Boston National League Baseball Club. He lived in Newtonville with his wife and at the time of the suit, served as a Director in the Commercial National Bank of Boston. Neighbors couldn't imagine Laura being involved in an illicit love affair with this man, or any other man for that matter. While the trial was pending, Frederick divorced his second wife. Small was awarded ten thousand dollars by Congressman Robert O. Harris, who served as auditor in the case. Harris limited the amount of damages awarded to Small to ten thousand dollars stating, "That the plaintiff was not a conniving party to her (his wife's) misconduct, but that he was an indifferent husband, who, after he knew that she was going wrong, was willing that she should, and ready to take advantage of any error she might make, either by way of obtaining a divorce or of making a profit."[3] Following the finalization of the divorce, Laura Patterson moved to New York, where she remained during Frederick's ordeal in Ossipee. Frederick Small spent the remainder of the year living alone in his Rogers Avenue house in Somerville. But shortly thereafter, he sold his house to move to the Curry farm in Southborough as the handyman.

The year that Small spent alone in Somerville was hardly spent in peaceful coexistence with his neighbors, since Small constantly argued with Mr. Jordan, the man who lived next door. Most of the arguments involved disagreements concerning properties. (It is interesting to note that Mr. Jordan had been the father of Chester Jordan, who was once employed as a vaudeville actor. Coincidentally, Chester Jordan was accused and convicted of murdering his wife, and spent his final days in a Massachusetts State Prison, before being executed in the electric chair. Frederick Small could only hope that the fate of Chester Jordan wasn't a mere foreshadowing of what was in store for his own future.)

Following his marriage to Florence and the loss of his position as handyman with the Currys, Frederick spent much of his time playing the stock market and making investments for himself and other acquaintances who trusted Small with their money. Small wound up losing a significant amount of his own money, as well as much of his friends' savings, in bucketshop plunges. Thus, the income that Small made from teaming up with Ed Connor to sell insurance to friends in the Boston area was deemed necessary to help support the Smalls' household, considering Frederick was semi-retired, and a good part of the money he had saved had been lost in the market.

Thus, the comfortable, tranquil, picturesque cottage on the shores of Lake Ossipee seemed to be destined to have been Florence and Frederick's final residence together. Separately, it may well have been their final home on earth. This was certainly the case for Florence; and barring an acquittal from the jury, Frederick would either be spending the rest of his life in jail, or he would be remanded into custody for a brief interval while awaiting execution. For although there were rumors of an upcoming motion from some of the members of the legislature to abolish capital punishment, the state of New Hampshire still had a death penalty on the books—death by hanging. But now it was out of Frederick's hands and up to the attorneys, the jury, and the evidence saved by the standing water in his cellar—the cellar which Mark Winkley's grandson insists would have been water tight had Frederick Small been willing to pay the price to have a cement floor poured.

[1] McLean, pg. 4.
[2] The State of New Hampshire Superior Court, *State vs. Frederick Small: Respondent's Bill of Exceptions,* Carroll County Courthouse, December Term, 1916, pg. 18.
[3] "Soden Must Pay $10,000," *New York Times,* April 28, 1911.

VII. THE CRIME

With the circumstantial case becoming stronger and stronger against Frederick Small, the prosecution was acutely aware they had to produce some form of incendiary device to fully incriminate the defendant. Without a timed fire-starting device, Frederick Small's alibi was airtight, and history of former spousal abuse was not enough to convict the man of murder. There were plenty of abusive, dysfunctional families known to authorities throughout New Hampshire where nobody turned up dead. Simply because a relationship was abusive didn't mean that participants were necessarily in a life-threatening situation.

Considering the fact that nothing was found on Small's person to directly link him to the crime, barring the meticulously written inventory and personal items that were thought to have been peculiar articles to accompany a man on an overnight business trip, there was no solid evidence that Small was involved in the murder. These items found in Small's satchel didn't prove involvement in the crime, they simply appeared to be strange, considering what occurred in Ossipee the night Small chose to take them with him. Instruments of murder found in the cottage ruins—such as the revolver, the cord, the fireplace poker, and the kerosene—were already present on the property, being used for common household purposes, and anyone who broke into the cottage could have used them.

The only proof the prosecution had that Florence was dead when Frederick Small left for his overnight to Boston was the fact that her stomach contained bits of undigested meat and vegetables, and it was pure speculation that the Smalls ate their dinner on September 28, 1916, around the noon hour, a meal that consisted of meat and vegetables. Nobody witnessed the Smalls eating their dinner that day except for Frederick Small himself, who insisted he and his wife ate a light meal of canned shrimp. This fact could only be disputed with the use of friends and neighbors establishing the habits of Florence and Frederick Small, by stating that they usually ate their heartiest meal at noontime. However, it came to the prosecution's attention that Dr. Carleton once witnessed the Smalls cooking a hearty meal, which included meat and vegetables, around the supper hour, just before dusk. Thus, the Smalls didn't habitually, 100% of the time, take their heartiest meal during the early afternoon. It was possible that Florence Small may have warmed over a bowl of soup or stew at the supper hour, as the defense team had speculated. Dr. Carleton's testimony couldn't be avoided at the upcoming trial since he was instrumental in performing an extensive examination of Florence's partially charred body. Yet his testimony concerning the Smalls' dining habits could potentially destroy the basis for the prosecution to prove beyond a reasonable doubt that Florence was dead when Frederick left for Boston.

Investigators had to have known that an impartial individual would have had no other recourse but to entertain reasonable doubt considering the prosecution's case thus far. An unbiased juror may not have cared for Frederick Small or most of the actions or deeds that had marked his life thus far, but there didn't seem to have been enough evidence to convict the man of murdering his wife. The prosecution needed a substantially stronger case. The reconstruction of an incendiary device was needed to establish a method for Frederick to set fire to his property approximately seven hours after leaving home for Boston.

During the preliminary hearing, a rough concept of an incendiary contraption, consisting of a candle floating on a block of wood in a container of kerosene, was volunteered as a possible method of starting a fire in a dwelling when the arsonist was some distance from the site. However, considering Small's substantial knowledge of electrical apparatus, the prosecution sought to reveal a more sophisticated device where the arsonist would have had more control over the timing of the event. With the German silver wire found in the cellar, along with a spark plug, some copper wiring, dry cells, kerosene, an alarm clock, and a coil, the prosecution worked with several mechanics and electricians to build a hypothetical incendiary device that could have been set to go off at a specific time after the cottage was abandoned.

However, during the preliminary search of the burned building, investigators noted some of the wires located in the ruins were found to lead under a coal pile in the Smalls' cellar. It would have been difficult to imagine that these wires were associated with an incendiary device. Furthermore, the German silver wire thought to have been linked to an incendiary device was believed to have originally been part of a hairbrush. Also, much of the wire found was telephone wire used in relocating phone lines, something that Small enjoyed doing in his spare time. As a matter of fact, in the kitchen the relocated phone wiring actually supported the stove pipe, which would account for the nails and the wire found in the basement. Furthermore, when these items were located in the burned out cottage, none were found to be joined together or connected in any manner. Despite all this conflicting information, all of these items were considered by the prosecution as possible elements of Frederick Small's incendiary device.

In anticipation of the necessity of proof, Franklin S. Piper, an electrician from Manchester, was consulted to build an incendiary device with elements similar to those found in the basement ruins. This device would hopefully model that which Small may have used to set his cottage on fire long after he had left for Boston. Piper used all the items except the spark plug, since it had a serious defect making it useless in igniting a fire. The particular device that Piper built was not terribly complicated and didn't require a great deal of mechanical knowledge. In fact, Piper felt that any schoolboy who was given the same materials could build this sort of device with little trouble. Piper described the device created as a "simple method of building an electrical fire kindler."[1]

Piper's experiments included the use of as little as one battery, to as many as six dry cells, to initiate a timed fire. He was successful in all cases. The batteries were connected to each other by wire similar to that found in Frederick Small's cellar. From the end battery, Piper carried a wire over to the alarm clock, and wrapped the wire around the alarm hand. Then Piper attached another wire to the hour hand of the clock, and carried this wire to a wire of greater resistance. For this, he used a series of German silver wires, again similar to those found in the cottage ruins. He attached yet another wire to the far end of the German silver wire, which led back to the series of batteries. The theory was that as the hour hand came around and connected with the alarm hand, the circuit would become complete, heating the German silver wire, and kindling a fire. As Piper tested his device, turning the hour hand to connect with the alarm hand, the German silver wire began to glow a brilliant red. It wasn't necessary for the hands to make a perfect connection; the important thing was that the hands met enough to complete the circuit, allowing current to flow into the German silver wire. Because it's more difficult for electrical current to move through German silver wire than through regular wire, heat would have been created, similar to the method by which heat is created in a toaster. All Small needed was a kerosene soaked cloth to act as a wick, and his fire would have been ignited. Piper concluded, "The wires would be burned off in half a second and the kindling of the fire would be done so quickly as to be invisible to the eye."[2]

An electrician and mechanical engineer from North Conway named Edwin Thompson was also consulted by the prosecution to devise a viable incendiary device. The device that Thompson produced was even simpler than Piper's, consisting of a set of batteries, an alarm clock, a zigzag set of wires similar to those found in a toaster, and a few ordinary kitchen matches. Both men were able to produce a timed fire without the use of a spark plug, therefore the dysfunction of the spark plug found in Small's cellar had little bearing on the case.

Dr. Bartley Carleton, who worked as a garage keeper in the Ossipee area, was intrigued by the idea of a possible incendiary device used to cover up the murder at the lakeside cottage. His interest led him to dabble in his own experiments, using materials similar to those which he played a significant role in finding on the morning of September 29 in the ruins of Frederick Small's basement. Some of his experiments failed; however many succeeded.

To set up the apparatus necessary to set such a fire, Dr. Carleton felt it would take "anywhere from a minute up."[3] Edwin Thompson added that after the apparatus was set up, a fire could be initiated within ten minutes. Thompson further advised that in order to produce even a simple incendiary device such as the one he had built, a man would have needed a reasonable amount of experience with electricity and would have had to run several tests of his equipment to make certain it would function as it should.

Franklin Piper, who more than anyone else qualified as an authority on the subject of electricity, would more than likely be selected as expert witness to lay the foundation for this area of the case against Frederick Small. Piper firmly believed a fire could have been set some seven hours after the defendant left his home using a device like the one he had built.

With a feasible incendiary device identified, prosecutors must have wondered about the eyewitness reports the sheriff collected just hours after the fire. Reports that the cottage appeared to have burned evenly, with an intense heat unlike any house fire previously experienced, didn't mesh with the type of fire the experimental devices were capable of creating. Investigators had to have known the devices they constructed were not capable of producing that impressive an inferno.

While sifting through the evidence, investigators noticed what appeared to have been melted iron on several pieces of metal recovered from the blaze. A section of stove pipe had melted, and a crusty residue remained along a part of the surface of the stove. In addition to the melted stove pipe, investigators found sections of melted iron on the Smalls' bed frame and bed spring.

After contacting a chemical and explosive expert named William F. Wedger from Massachusetts' District Court, investigators learned that it was highly likely that a strong chemical compound called thermit was used in addition to the incendiary device. Yet an incendiary device was still necessary to start the blaze, since thermit wasn't capable of igniting on its own. Nevertheless thermit, which was a chemical commonly used in welding trolley car rails and heavy pieces of machinery such as locomotive frames and the hulls of vessels, had the capability of burning with intense heat. This was one of its most attractive qualities because with the use of thermit, it was possible to weld machinery as it stood, with great speed, without the painstaking task of having to take down the pieces of machinery in order to work on them. In most situations, thermit had the capability to burn at approximately 5,200 degrees Fahrenheit, a much hotter temperature than the ten to eleven hundred degrees Fahrenheit that William Wedger estimated a wood fire could have been expected to burn. The melting point of iron is about 2,800 degrees. Thermit's capability of reaching 5,200 degrees in under one minute demonstrates the ease by which thermit could have burned through Mrs. Small's elbow and knee joints as well as the frame of her bed. This chemical composed of iron oxide and metallic aluminum, which is commonly placed under a layer of magnesia ignition powder, had the unique ability to melt metal in one area, yet leave an area two to three feet from that section unblemished. After examining the evidence, Walter Wedger was relatively certain that thermit had been present in some manner in the house fire.

But the prosecution was never able to take this piece of information much further, since although thermit was a popular welding compound, it was not easy to come by. Though Frederick Small was proven to have had a good working knowledge of electricity and phone wiring, welding was never considered to have been an interest of Small's. With no connection to welding or link to anyone working in welding, it was difficult to ascertain exactly how Small would have known about the substance, much less secure some for his own personal use.

Nevertheless, the use of thermit in the house fire by the arsonist, whatever his identity, could easily have explained how all the evidence wound up in a pool of water in the cellar, rather than being destroyed in the inferno, which was surely the intended scheme. A circle of thermit may have been placed around the bed on the second floor, and another pile of thermit may have been scattered on the stove in close proximity to the incendiary device in the kitchen. With the ignition of the fire, the thermit would have had an explosive quality, igniting a good portion of the kerosene-soaked first floor instantaneously. This would have accounted for the reason the house burned as uniformly as it did. The circle around the bed would have quickly ignited and burned a hole through the bedroom floor so rapidly that it would not have had time to burn the evidence placed on and around the bed. The bed and its contents could conceivably have dropped through the second floor into the first with such intensity that the impact and the hot burning fire would have quickly broken through the already weakened first story's floor, sending the evidence into the cellar, where the standing water quickly doused the flames. This would explain the eyewitness account the night of the fire, of briefly observing a woman's body on a bed on the first floor, then its sudden disappearance when he returned from trying to gain entry through the side door. The only fire remaining in the basement was the smoldering body of Florence Small, slowly burning with the aid of the water resistant resin that had been rubbed into her corpse. However, with no indication of any link to Frederick Small, the use of thermit in this fire couldn't be proved, even though the evidence fit the manner in which the cottage burned. For if the prosecution proved beyond a shadow of a doubt that thermit was used without providing evidence linking Small to the compound, this would only serve to prove Frederick Small's innocence rather than his guilt. Unless another suspect was found with knowledge of and access to the chemical compound, its use would never be proven in a court of law, and the mystery of the thermit would be forever hidden in the basement of Frederick Small's abandoned property.

[1] "Head of Murder Victim on View in Court Room," *The Manchester Leader and Evening Union*, Jan. 4, 1917, pg. 9.

[2] Ibid., pg. 9.

[3] "Direct Case Against Small Nears Completion," *The Manchester Leader and Evening Union*, Jan. 3, 1917, pg. 2.

VIII. THE TRIAL

Frederick Small spent the remainder of the Fall of 1916 in custody in the Carroll County jailhouse, with the sheriff keeping a watchful eye over the prisoner. By Christmas, there were two other prisoners under the sheriff's supervision, and the men ate Christmas dinner in each other's company.

In Ossipee, Christmas 1916 was overshadowed by the impending trial to begin on December 26 at 2:00 P.M. with jury selection. A change of venue had not been granted for Frederick Small and his attorneys, William S. Matthews and Sidney F. Stevens of Somersworth, and Sewell Abbott of Wolfboro, who notably often wore a vivid pink posie in his buttonhole. A panel of eighty-two men had been notified of their duty to appear at the Carroll County Courthouse to potentially serve as jurors for this monumental case. The proceeding had gained the distinction of being the first important trial to be held in the brand new Carroll County Courthouse, and its significance was surely destined to go down in history. The hotels and inns within the area of Ossipee were totally insufficient to accommodate the massive number of people who would be staying and working in town, serving in a number of different capacities. Shortly before Christmas, all of the rooms in and around Ossipee had been reserved, and the hotel managers spent most of their time on Christmas Day trying to arrange for accommodations in private homes.

On the opening day of the trial, newspapers reported that Ossipee was as "crowded as a rush hour trolley."[1] It wasn't just lawyers and clerks who were cramming into the little, country town. This murder had become a common topic of conversation in places as far away as Boston, Massachusetts, and Portland, Maine, not to mention its notoriety within the state of New Hampshire itself. The trial, of course, had become an expected sensation, and lawyers, witnesses, prospective jurors, correspondents, political dignitaries such as senators and representatives, and just plain spectators were all there to see the fate of the graying Boston broker sealed. By now, people were voluntarily committing themselves to the county jail, in order to have a place to stay. One Ossipee resident was noted to say, "there are no billiard rooms here, or they would have become improvised dormitories."[2]

Life for Frederick Small, however, was somewhat less than fulfilling. He continued to maintain his innocence, even though newspapers were reporting that at his preliminary hearing, Small's council offered no defense for him. Small had gained weight during his three month confinement in jail, which his attorneys implied was a sign of confidence that it indicated "an absence of worry over the outcome of the trial."[3] Small's spirits rose each day at the prospect of attending his trial, and he never wavered in his confidence that he would receive an acquittal and walk out of the courthouse a free man.

The presiding judge was John Kivel, and the state's prosecution team consisted of two men, Attorney General James P. Tuttle and County Solicitor Walter T. Hill. Of these two men, James Tuttle was the most notable to the Boston papers, not for his flamboyant gift of oration or his brilliant interpretation of the law, although that is not to say that he didn't possess these qualities. No, James P. Tuttle was most noted for his, "old-fashioned chin whiskers and . . . . his trousers stuffed into cowhide boots."[4] For the sophisticated readers of the Boston newspapers, James Tuttle was described as the perfect representation of "a cartoon of a country hick."[5] However, Ossipee jurors liked Tuttle, and he was considered a good man in those parts.

With the state's prosecution team submitting a witness list of nearly 100 names, the prosecution and Small's defense team began the tedious task of selecting suitable jurors for the trial. Of the eighty-two men examined for service to the jury, only seventy-two were questioned. Many of these men were excused because they had formed a previous opinion in the case. However neither the defense nor the prosecution used all of the peremptory challenges available to them.

The local papers were to report that Judge Kivel, whose reputation in Carroll County was second to none, had decided to employ a new method of choosing a jury. This process was thought to be expedient, fair, impartial, and expeditious, since there were so many men to sort through to find twelve suitable jurors. Under this new procedure, each of the seventy-two men were called to the witness stand and asked a number of questions concerning their age, their amount of reading concerning the subject matter of the trial, and any opinions formed about the case, Small's attorneys, or Small and his wife. And as in the last notable murder trial in the state of New Hampshire, the Peaslee case, all potential jurors were asked about their feelings concerning the death penalty. If Judge Kivel was content with the responses, he would qualify the man for jury service, whereby attorneys had the opportunity to ask further questions, or to accept or challenge the selection of the man as juror. By 4:30, after fielding questions concerning their feelings about capital punishment, their church membership, and their use of liquor, five jurors had been selected for service. Four of these jurors were under the age of forty, the youngest being thirty-three years old. They all hailed from the local and surrounding areas. Frederick Small was an active participant in these proceedings, as he often crossed names off the prospective juror list before his attorney had even finished his questioning. At the end of the day, those men selected for jury duty were placed under the supervision of the sheriff's deputies, John Quimby and Arthur Tuttle. Those men not yet examined were allowed to catch a train to return home for the night.

On the following day, James Welch, one of the remaining men not yet examined by the court, disembarked the train from Tamworth. While Welch walked toward the courthouse, he was met by a local storekeeper named Ausbry Moulton.

"Where's your grip?"[6] Moulton called out to Welch.

"It's home,"[7] Welch replied, thinking this to be a strange question, considering he hadn't so much as been interviewed by the court.

As Moulton greeted Welch, he quickly explained the meaning of his peculiar question. It seemed that during the night, Moulton overheard the lawyers talking about the men remaining on the list who had not yet been examined. Moulton told Welch, "There is twenty of you fellows that both sides will accept, and you are one of the twenty."[8] At that, James telephoned his home from Ausbry's store to be sure his things were sent directly to the courthouse. As it turned out, Welch was the seventh juror selected that day. Of the twelve jurors, eight were local farmers, three were carpenters, and one was a stationary engineer. Their ages ranged from thirty to fifty-one, with eight of the jurors falling in the thirty to thirty-nine year old category. Because most of the seasonal residents around Lake Ossipee were registered to vote in their place of winter residencies; for Carroll County, this was the closest the court system could get to a jury of Frederick Small's peers. The *Manchester Leader* best summed up the essence of the jury with its headline on December 27, "Carroll County farmers will decide guilt or innocence of Boston man charged with murder of wife at Mountainview on September 28."[9]

The jury was sequestered for the entire trial, a trial that newspapers reported could take as long as three weeks, with an anticipated five witnesses taking the stand each day. To assure the jury was totally sequestered, a supply of padlocks and nails were used to secure their rooms. The jurors were instructed that they were not to read the newspapers, however, old magazines would be supplied to occupy their time. Communication with anyone from the outside was firmly prohibited, and the contents of any written communication to or from families had to be examined by a court officer before being sent or received. Jurors were warned not to talk among themselves about the case until the evidence was closed and deliberations had commenced. Finally, jurors were advised to watch their diet and their health, since illness among the jurors could result in causing the disqualification of the trial, necessitating a new trial. Several special deputies were sworn into service specifically to help out with extra duties deriving from the Small trial. According to James Welch, "Every juror was keyed up at the start, for such a thing had never come within 100 miles of us up here, but as the trial went on, the tension let down. You must remember that we twelve men had Small's life in our hands and we felt the responsibility. It's no fun playing God."[10]

The jury took up residency in the Carroll Inn for the duration of the trial, where four rooms had been reserved for their stay. A woman from the area named Mrs. Merrow was one of the special deputies sworn in by the courts to prepare the jurors' meals and take care of the housekeeping of their rooms. Because of the lack of exercise the jurors would endure for the next three weeks, the court cautioned Mrs. Merrow not to provide too much hearty food or large servings. The physical state of the jurors was a significant concern to the court, and every attempt was made to keep the jurors healthy.

With the jury seated, a recess for lunch was taken, followed by an unprecedented and rather hurried escort to the scene of the crime prior to opening statements. A heavy snow was predicted for the Ossipee region of New Hampshire, which could have potentially hampered the ability of the jurors to assess the crime scene if they had waited. Thus, following Harry Sawyer's presentation of the plans of the Small cottage, the jury was escorted approximately five miles to the crime scene. A large pung that was drawn by four horses pulled up in front of the courthouse, which the jurors boarded for their trip to the cottage ruins. Frederick Small and his guards were taken to the location in a smaller, horse-drawn sleigh. Cars were provided by the court for the judge, council, and the official stenographer. Even the newspaper correspondents became a part of the caravan, following in cars they had driven up from the city. It was a grand procession, unlike any the small town of Ossipee had seen before.

As they approached the ruins of the cottage, Frederick Small began weeping. The sheriff supported Small as they walked over to the blackened spot where Frederick's home once stood. As his eyes settled on the charred ruins, Small sobbed uncontrollably. The county solicitor, Walter D. Hill, did not waiver, however, as he proceeded to point out the positioning of the doors of the Small cottage and the location of neighboring dwellings. Making his way over to the location of what had once been Small's workshop, Hill pointed out the area where the side door had once stood. Then, he directed the jury's attention to the place where Florence's body had been discovered and the position of the revolver as it related to the location of the body. From the start Walter Hill made a favorable impression on the jurors. James Welch reminisced, "He would get the facts of the case so nice and neat that the witness didn't realize he had told everything he knew."[11] Because of this attribute, Hill assisted the State's case by performing most of the questioning of the prosecution's witnesses.

When the county solicitor had concluded, the defense attorney, Sydney Stevens, asked the jury to focus their attention on a hatchway door that led from the outside of the house, down a flight of stairs, to the cellar. Stevens especially noted the latch that was on the inside of the door that served as a fastener. The young, bright attorney pointed out that when this latch was in an unlocked position, the paint had barely been touched. The rest of the door was severely charred and damaged by the flames. Stevens was hoping to apply this discovery to the defense theory that a tramp had broken into the cottage while Frederick was away, had killed Florence, had set the fire, then had escaped through this unlocked hatchway door. In keeping with this theory, Stevens also asked the jury to note the lonely mile long road that led through the woods before finally connecting with the main thoroughfare to the town of Ossipee. Also noted were the uninhabited cottages in the vicinity, whose seasonal residents had left weeks before the murder. Before returning to the courthouse, the jury continued to the center of Mountainview, where they boarded a train to give them a feel for the route that Frederick Small covered on that fateful day in September.

Opening statements began on the morning of December 28, with Walter Hill summarizing the murder of Florence Small as being "one of the foulest and most brutal murders in the annals of crime."[12] Hill gave a brief introduction to evidence linked to the fire, the insurance policy, the accounts of abuse, the items found in the ruins of the cottage, and the contents of Small's satchel which accompanied him to Boston. Soon a web of circumstantial evidence had been spun, with the promise of testimony not previously made public, to add to the intrigue of the trial. Although Frederick Small, from the day he was taken into custody, seemed almost stoic in nature, he once again cried steadily while the court clerk read the indictment. When the passage concerning the legal description of the crime was read, Small sobbed uncontrollably.

While all this was taking place in the little town of Ossipee, lawmakers in New Hampshire's state capital of Concord were busy introducing important legislation that related to the death penalty. This legislation called for the abolishment of the capital punishment clause included in the murder law for the state of New Hampshire. Although this legislation could have had a crucial influence on the fate of Frederick Small, since he was being tried for a capital offense, it came too late to alter any decision that was to be handed down in his murder trial in Carroll County. Deliberations on the bill were not begun until March 21, 1917. If Frederick Small were to be found guilty, he would have to depend on the statement of most jurors who were interviewed that concluded, "they were opposed on general principles to capital punishment and only the most conclusive evidence would induce them to bring a recommendation for the death penalty for a convicted defendant."[13]

December 28, 1916 also marked the day that Florence's mother, Mrs. Elizabeth Curry, and her sister, Miss Norma Curry, arrived back in Ossipee. Although it was well known that the two women had dinner at the hotel with Ex-Police Inspector Andy Houghton, who served as their escort, and Alexander W. Clark, the policy registrar for John Hancock Mutual Life Insurance Company, the Currys gave no statement to the press. Both women were scheduled to testify at Frederick Small's murder trial, and would have gone against a court order if they spoke publicly outside of court.

On the first day the Currys were present in Ossipee, the courtroom was packed, even though it was December and the weather was cold and snowy. Small's brother was present in the courtroom, although he wasn't seen speaking to Small at all. It was understood that Frederick and his brother hadn't spoken to each other in years. The basement of the courthouse had been turned into a reporters' room, where a special wire to Boston was open for twenty-four hour usage. Twenty or more reporters were said to have been using the workspace at a time.

As witnesses began to testify, much of the day's records centered around the many stories of verbal abuse that Frederick Small leveled toward his wife. George Emerson spoke of the card game when Florence misdealt a hand and Frederick launched such a verbal attack on his wife that she was reduced to tears. George's wife then took the stand to verify that she heard a woman's scream coming from the Smalls' house shortly after the break-up of the card game.

The next testimony was given by Mr. Davis, the Smalls' mailman and milkman. Davis spoke of several instances when he observed Fred Small abusing his wife, which led defense attorney, Mr. Matthews, to jump to his feet and object to the line of questioning. The prosecution responded with a shift in subject for the time being, since Mr. Davis helped to establish the fact that the side door, from which Small exited his cottage for the final time, was equipped with a spring lock. But Davis was helpful to Mr. Matthews and the defense team as well in establishing the direction in which the side door swung. As a matter of fact, Matthews repeated Davis's answer three times for effect, before dropping the subject. It would be up to the defense to prove the door lock was an old-fashioned style that needed to be locked from the inside by Florence after Frederick left the house. Everyone felt this door would play a significant role in the trial, although some weren't quite certain how it figured into the case. Davis's testimony resulted in the lawyers for both sides taking a short recess to discuss the attorney general's line of questioning in chambers. When they returned, the information concerning the lock and the door was allowed, but Tuttle was warned to discontinue his line of questioning concerning Small's "domineering attitude"[14] toward his wife.

Ed Connor's daughter, Helen, testified next, stating that once when she was complimenting Florence on her wonderful cooking skills, Frederick replied, "sometimes I have to take an axe to her."[15] Mary Conner followed her daughter, to speak of Frederick's use of vulgar language toward Florence when she couldn't steer the motorboat with a cord he had arranged. According to Mrs. Conner, the cord was notable because it was composed of a "slender fabric"[16] which was similar to the cord she was shown at the doctor's office shortly after Florence's murder. Lilla Ferren testified that Florence often spoke of how lonely she was at her isolated lakeside cottage. However, after the jury had the opportunity to hear all this testimony, it was excluded from the record due to the disallowed line of questioning.

During the morning's testimony, Frederick Small remained seated with his coat on and his collar turned up close to his neck. The new courthouse was chilly, especially in the early morning hours. When the heat finally began to circulate around the room,

Small turned his collar down and sat more comfortably. Frederick listened intently to the testimony, and displayed no hint of emotion throughout the day's proceedings—that is, until Mr. Davis gave his testimony. At that time, several witnesses in the courtroom noticed Small cast a cynical smile toward Davis, which he tried to cover with his hand. Notably, this response from Small occurred at the time that Davis was relaying his hunting trip story, in which Frederick tried to hit Florence over the head with an oar for grounding the boat on a sandbar. Small clearly felt the day's accounts of abuse were trivial, and in fact, fairly amusing. He, as well as his attorneys, believed that these accounts had little to do with the crime for which he was standing trial.

The remainder of the day's testimony centered around the $20,000 life insurance policy that was considered to have been the primary motive for the murder. A fire insurance policy had also been taken out on the cottage and its contents for the sum of $3,000, which was far more than the property was actually worth. Special attention was given to the fact that Frederick Small had, at first, illegally signed Florence's name to the documents, and was reluctant to discuss the policy with Florence. The fact that annual premiums for the two policies amounted to $1,107.60, which was approximately 25% of Small's total savings, further added suspicion that Small had planned to collect on these policies sooner rather than later.

The following day of testimony traced the steps of Frederick Small on September 28. Charles Sceggel and George Kennett reluctantly told of their experiences with Small on that day. They testified reluctantly because both men felt friendly towards Small; George Kennett even having a snifter with him whenever he was called to drive Frederick somewhere. Both men felt a sort of loyalty to Small, and testifying made them uncomfortable. Ed Conner also testified concerning his trip to Boston and the sudden change of plans for the business trip. The postcard that Small wrote with Ed while in Boston was placed into evidence. Ed told of the call from Ossipee and Frederick's response, and of the car ride home. Connor also spoke of finding the body of Florence Small in the cellar of the cottage, and dousing the flames that were still smoldering.

The proceedings on December 30 began with the testimony of Andrew Houghton, who gave a detailed description of the circumstances surrounding the death threat he overheard Frederick hurl at Florence in a Boston courtroom. Sewell Abbott performed the cross-examination of Houghton, specifically dwelling on the fact that Houghton told nobody of the threatening remark following the incident. Abbott was alluding to the fact that the remark couldn't have seemed too life threatening at the time or he would have reported the incident to somebody. In his own defense, Houghton volunteered the information that Norma Curry also heard the remark, and Abbott replied, "Oh yes,"[17] and quickly ended his line of cross-examination.

Following Houghton's testimony, the prosecution shifted gears somewhat to enter into evidence the household inventory found in Small's satchel the morning he returned to Ossipee. Most notable concerning the meticulously written listing was the absence of any mention of the revolver found in the cellar of the burned out cottage and the $6,000 worth of jewelry Small professed to have owned. Ed Connor took the stand to verify that the writing on the inventory was Small's, and he identified the revolver as being one similar to a gun Small had owned. Mary Connor and Lilla Ferrin were recalled to the stand to identify three rings and a watch that had belonged to Florence Small.

As the day wore on, Dr. Bacon, who had traveled all the way from Southborough, Massachusetts, to testify on the Currys' behalf, took the stand. The prosecution first posed questions concerning a clock that Frederick Small had devised to illuminate at night while residing at the Currys' farm. As the prosecution began a new line of testimony, the defense sensed that another attempt to establish their client's abusive nature toward his wife was about to come up, and they immediately asked to speak in chambers with the judge and the prosecution. The defense was trying to keep the jury from hearing the account of abuse, as they had heard previous allegations of abuse in this trial. Even though these previous remarks were stricken from the record and the jury was instructed not to consider this information, the damage was done. The testimony concerning the confrontation in the kitchen of the Curry farm in Southborough, when Frederick hit his new bride over the head with a bootjack and threatened Dr. Bacon with a log, would have left a lasting impression with the jury. Following a lengthy conference in chambers, however, the defense was successful in squelching this information in court.

Frank Ferrin was called to the stand next to give his account of the precise wording of the phone conversation he had with Small the night of the fire. Frank also testified concerning extraordinary features of that particular cottage fire, which he hadn't previously observed in any other fire. Frank also testified that while viewing the burned cottage the next morning, Small momentarily walked down to the beach and took a tape measure from his pocket to measure the size of some tracks he had found in the sand. These footprints had been perceived by the prosecution as irrelevant, although Small appeared to have believed they would become a factor in the case at some point.

Continuing the steady flow of witnesses on this afternoon of December 30 was Mr. Jaynes from Lynn, Massachusetts. His accounts of Small's use of profanity when addressing his wife and screams resounding from the Smalls' cottage at night seemed anticlimactic, since the family's dysfunction was well established. However, Horace Davis's testimony added new information concerning Small's treatment of his wife. Davis, who was a mason by trade, was working in Small's cellar when he overheard Norma Curry tell Frederick that she felt he was responsible for her sister's illness. Frederick answered her rather snidely when he said, "You have not been invited here and might leave."[18] Florence needed Norma's help at that time, since she was too ill to care for herself and her home, so Norma didn't pursue the issue. However, Horace Davis claimed that Frederick didn't deny the accusation.

With that, the court recessed for the night. Because December 31 was a Sunday, court was not in session. However, jurors were treated to a two-mile hike, as Judge Kivel wanted to be sure the men received enough exercise to stay healthy. Jim Welch's characterization of their Sunday's activities as being, "taken out for exercise,"[19] brings to mind a dog or a horse, rather than a person.

There was no holiday from court on Monday, January 1, 1917. Frederick Small met the New Year with confidence that in 1917, he would be acquitted, and cleared of the crime which had robbed him of his freedom. Judge Kivel, the attorneys, and witnesses scheduled to appear in court the next day were compelled to stay overnight in

Ossipee, rather than returning to their homes for New Year's Eve. Judge Kivel had become concerned that Small's trial wasn't progressing as quickly as he had hoped. Originally he had anticipated the prosecution resting on Saturday. As things were going, it looked as though the prosecution's case wouldn't rest until Tuesday at the earliest. However, that was not to say that Judge Kivel heralded the New Year alone, as it was noted by the local press that he entertained an old friend from Dartmouth College named Charles Whitcomb, who stayed to observe the court proceedings the following day.

The New Year brought forth a shocking line of exhibits. Much to the protest and objection of the defense, Florence's skull, clothing worn at the time of the murder, and pieces of the cord used to strangle Florence were all submitted into evidence. Judge Kivel advised the women in attendance to leave the courtroom while the skull was on display. Most women abided by the judge's wishes. Florence's skull remained on display for two to three days, and a jar containing Mrs. Small's stomach and its contents sat on a table beside her skull. However, Florence's partially burned clothing and bloodstained bedding were kept in the courthouse basement and not publicly displayed.

Dr. Hodsdon testified that he and Medical Referee B. Frank Horne found the cord around Mrs. Small's neck after lifting what appeared to have been a cloth mask off the face of the victim. Subsequent tests showed the cloth was covered with a mixture of grease and resin, which in all probability was placed on the body to assure its total disintegration in the fire. Physical evidence demonstrated that the trauma to the head and throat of Florence Small was brutal. The cord had actually cut into the throat of the woman, leaving a wound half as deep as the cord was wide. The force of such a severe strangulation actually caused Florence's tongue to protrude from her mouth. However, Dr. Hodsdon agreed that in a death by suffocation, such as in a fire, the tongue also may protrude from the mouth of a victim. The marks on the side of Florence's skull were evidence that she was beaten with the butt end of a fireplace poker. As proof, Dr. Hodsdon took the fireplace poker found in the ruins and matched it to indentations in Florence's skull. Three cuts in her skull were said to have been produced by several blows to the head with the sharp end of a coal-slicing bar.

Indications of strangulation and beatings were almost over-shadowed by evidence of a bullet wound in Mrs. Small's skull. The bullet was thought to have entered Florence's head above her left eye, shattering the hinge of her right jaw, where it became lodged in her jaw bone. It appeared that the shooter was standing over Florence when the .32 caliber revolver was fired, as the angle of the entry wound demonstrated. Dr. Hodsdon conceded, the bullet wound would have been fatal, but Florence actually died from strangulation. Although her body was set on fire and most of the front was severely burned, miraculously Florence's back was only slightly discolored, leaving her heart, lungs, and other internal organs intact. Following examination by Doctor Horne at Dartmouth, Mrs. Small's organs were sent to Dr. George Magrath, the medical examiner for Suffolk County in Boston, to undergo analysis.

Dr. Magrath's testimony echoed the testimony of Dr. Hodsdon. According to Dr. Magrath, Florence's head had all the appearances consistent with a death by strangulation. Dr. Magrath used a probe to trace the path the bullet took, to help the jury understand the medical examiner's conclusion that when shot, Florence was prostrate with the shooter standing over her, to her left. The wounds on Florence's skull were not said to have been fatal blows. Further, Dr. Magrath confirmed that the bullet wound probably would have been fatal, if the strangulation had not occurred. However, death would not have been instantaneous from the bullet wound.

As Dr. Magrath testified, Frederick Small sat with a good part of his face covered by a handkerchief. When Florence's skull was exhibited, Small squirmed uneasily in his seat. His face was reddened during the entire testimony, and Small was visibly shaken. However, few people in the courtroom noticed Small's reactions because their attention was riveted to the skull on exhibit and the words of the doctor.

Following Dr. Magrath's grizzly testimony, the jury had to have been relieved when questioning shifted focus to the fire and the hatchway door leading to the basement. Elmer Loring took the stand to speak about his initial observations of the fire. Because his cottage was closest to the Smalls' house, Loring was one of the first men on the scene. He testified that the fire seemed to be, "burning all over at once."[20] Loring was certain the hatchway door leading to the basement would not open when he and another man desperately tried to gain entry to the burning building. As he struggled with the door, Loring felt the hatchway had to have been locked from the inside. Loring's statement would seem to shatter the defense theory that an intruder escaped through the hatchway door, leaving the latch in an unfastened position, as scorch marks left on the door had indicated.

The final testimony of the day covered information not yet mentioned by authorities. This new information established the fact that neighbors observed there were no lights turned on in the Small cottage on the evening of the murder and subsequent fire. Specifically, George Glover and Arthur Boynton of Melrose, Massachusetts, made this claim, a claim that was left undisputed by the defense. With many new pieces of evidence for jurors to mull over, the court adjourned for the night.

As court proceedings for January 2 advanced, headlines declared that Small would take the stand on his own behalf. Reporters interviewed Small daily, at which time he professed his innocence and his confidence that he would be exonerated of all wrongdoing. Reporters were struck by the fearless nature Small demonstrated throughout the trial. He showed no signs of worry concerning the trial's outcome from its commencement, and was actively involved. For example, when Ed Connor was explaining some charts to the court, Small rose from his seat and limped over to get a closer look at the papers. Frederick also took detailed notes while the prosecution's witnesses were on the stand, and Small would often confer with his council when they were cross-examining these witnesses. From all appearances, an unknowing spectator may have thought Small was one of the lawyers on the defense team. However when the scalp of his murdered wife was placed on top of her skull and passed by each member of the jury for observation, Small wept. Frederick Small, from all appearances, was the portrait of an innocent man, or an extremely confident man without a conscience.

The morning's testimony presented information concerning Florence's stomach contents, and their relationship to the time of her death. Several witnesses were called to verify the time of day the Smalls took their main meal, although the defense continued to emphasize that the Smalls ate canned shrimp for lunch the day of the murder. The defense asserted that Florence must have warmed over some soup or stew for her evening meal, shortly before being attacked.

Sheriff Chandler unveiled several more articles to be introduced into evidence—a spark plug, some wires, nails, a revolver and shells. The diaries and letters from Small's satchel were also entered into evidence, at which time Judge Kivel ordered the contents of the two letters be suppressed and not revealed to the public. These two letters were written in 1908 and 1909 by Laura Patterson, Small's second wife. Upon cross-examination concerning the revolver, the sheriff told the court that although he found several .32 caliber shells when he searched the basement of the cottage, he was only able to locate one empty shell, and that was of a larger caliber. This testimony directly conflicted with headlines from the October 3, 1916 *Manchester Union* article confirming that an empty shell was recovered which matched the caliber pistol found in the ruins. Chandler also had to recant his original testimony concerning Small's strong desire to gain access to his satchel when he returned from Boston. When pressed on the subject, the sheriff admitted that Small made no real determined effort to take possession of his satchel after his arrest. Chandler also conceded that Frederick Small easily agreed to a voluntary search of his pockets upon returning to Ossipee.

Never before had the townspeople of Ossipee been more captivated by the comings and goings of strangers in town. Folks attempted to put a name to every face in town and speculated about those new faces that couldn't be identified. The *Manchester Leader* noted this phenomenon when it stated, "The specific general rumors are those which bring Small's second wife into the case, and which create identities for more or less mysterious witnesses who come and go like phantoms in the night."[21] Folks in town were especially interested in tracing the footsteps of Dr. Magrath and Professor Wedger, who enjoyed a walk in the mountains from time to time. Magrath and Wedger professed to enjoy the fresh, clean mountain air. Yet speculation as to what these two learned men spoke about while on their hikes ran rampant, since it was thought that they were using the walks to discuss new theories about the case.

When court resumed on January 3, Dr. Bartley Carleton was the first witness to take the stand. Dr. Carleton testified to the condition of Florence's body when first recovered, noting that he was responsible for removing the cord from her neck. Carleton then proceeded to give a demonstration to the jury of how Small tied the cord around Florence's throat, a cord which bore a perfectly formed square knot, resting precisely at the center of the back of Florence's neck.

Following the demonstration, Dr. Carleton was asked a question by the prosecution which, in time, would be repeated for two other witnesses. "Assuming that you have a spark plug and copper wires, an alarm clock, a coil, three to six dry cell batteries, gasoline or kerosene; with this material could a fire be produced to start at any time within ten hours ahead?"[22] The defense was on its feet instantly. Matthews disputed the allowance of evidence into the trial concerning any form of incendiary device. When the judge's ruling was unfavorable to the defense, they further objected on the grounds that Dr. Carleton wasn't an expert witness. However it was decided that Dr. Carleton worked enough with coils, batteries, and wires in his garage to give an educated opinion on the subject. Dr. Carleton, as well as Dr. Hodsdon and Franklin Piper, the other two witnesses to whom this question was posed, all agreed that a timed fire could be started using these items. However, the witnesses disagreed on the speed in which the incendiary device could be set up and set off.

Dr. Hodsdon and Dr. Carleton also disagreed on the amount of time it would have taken to carry out the murders. Dr. Hodsdon felt it would have taken the murderer about five minutes for the attack on Florence Small. Dr. Carleton, on the otherhand, estimated it would have taken about twenty minutes for the entire murder to have taken place. The key to the timing of the assaults would have been linked to how prepared the murderer was to commit the assaults. However, Dr. Hodsdon stated the murder happened in about three minutes, since that was how long it would have taken Florence to succumb to strangulation with a cord wrapped so tightly around her neck.

The remainder of the day was used to define and demonstrate the kind of incendiary device Frederick Small used to set his cottage on fire while he was away on a business trip to Boston. The purchase of an electrical handbook by Small, the prosecution contended, was another indication Small was working on a device to set his cottage on fire. During the cross-examination of this testimony, however, there was confusion as to whether a spark plug was used in the construction of the fire-setting device. Although the prosecution was unsure whether the spark plug had been used in setting the fire, they were able to prove, through the expert testimony of Franklin Piper, that a viable incendiary device could have been built without the use of a spark plug, using other materials found in the ruins.

The day's testimony ended with J. H. Fitzgerald, a firearms expert from Boston. Fitzgerald was able to pinpoint the sale of the revolver to Frederick Small, testifying that Small purchased the gun in Boston in 1911. Fitzgerald also identified the type of bullet taken from Florence's right jawbone as being one similar to that which would have been fired from an automatic revolver like the one recovered from the fire. With that, court adjourned until January 4, and Frederick Small was once more escorted back to jail.

The trial of Frederick Small was somewhat overshadowed by the inauguration of Henry Wilder Keyes, the new governor of New Hampshire, on January 4. The inauguration was noted as having the largest attendance of all inaugurations that had taken place to date. However, notably missing was Attorney General Tuttle, since he had a defendant to prosecute. Judge Kivel was taking no holidays that could result in an extension of this already long trial. For every day the trial was extended, there was a chance of a juror's illness or an emergency which could have resulted in the necessity of starting the trial over. With this as one of Judge Kivel's greatest fears, he worked to expedite the trial whenever possible. If the attorney general wished to witness the inauguration, he would have to do so vicariously through the newspapers.

While Governor-Elect Keyes was being sworn into office, focus in Ossipee shifted once more to the possible use of an incendiary device to start a fire in the cottage hours following Small's departure. The possibility of the use of the chemical compound thermit was introduced by Walter L. Wedger. However the defense moved that Wedger's testimony be stricken from the records. The defense reasoned that Frederick Small had not been linked to the chemical compound, as it was difficult to obtain. The defense argued further that none of the substance had been found. It was only the prosecution's speculation that this substance caused the intense heat of the fire that night.

The prosecution continued its case with the introduction of a checkbook into evidence to make the point that Small's funds were significantly depleted. They also read a number of entries from Small's diaries concerning the purchase price of many of the items included on Small's three page inventory. Each corresponding item reflected an approximate increase in value of at least 25% per item. The prosecution sought to prove by this testimony that Frederick Small was not only in need of money, it seemed that his intent was to inflate the value of his household inventory to receive a larger payoff from his insurance policy than he was entitled.

The prosecution then recalled Dr. Magrath to speak about the condition of Mrs. Small's internal organs. Dr. Magrath stated that Florence was free of any disease, and her organs demonstrated no sign of injury. However, because of the severe burning on the front side of her body, there was no way of knowing what kind of injuries below the neck, if any, Florence Small suffered in the course of the murder. This completed the medical testimony.

When Florence Small's skull and stomach contents were removed from display, the ladies were readmitted to the court-room. What followed was the much anticipated testimony of Miss Norma Curry and her mother, Mrs. Elizabeth Curry. Mrs. Curry was the first to testify. Elizabeth Curry immediately acquired the sympathy of all present in the courthouse as she recalled the day she was asked to confirm the identity of her de-ceased daughter's body through the recognition of a few strands of her hair. Mrs. Curry also spoke of a package that Frederick had wrapped for her whose strings bore a perfectly tied square knot. During cross-examination, the defense attempted to dem-onstrate that Elizabeth Curry might be unreliable in recogniz-ing various kinds of knots. Mrs. Curry explained that she was well-versed in identifying different knots. She further stated that her husband, "was a ship owner and master mariner and had shown her many varieties and kinds of knots."[23]

Norma Curry's testimony was the final testimony of the day, when among other things, she told of Small's ability to run telephone wiring. All of the relocated telephones on their farm in Southborough worked well, according to Norma. As a matter of fact, one day Frederick Small was boasting of his talent, holding his right hand straight up in the air, and stating, "That hand can do anything!"[24] The defense objected to the implications of admitting Small's statement. However, Judge Kivel ruled that the statement could stand, noting it only implies Small's belief in his own ingenuity, and nothing more.

Norma testified further that she had come to visit Florence from October 9 to October 12, 1915, when her sister had taken ill, at which time Norma performed the household duties. Their heartiest meal was always eaten at noontime, as Frederick preferred to eat following his morning's work. Norma recognized the alarm clock found in the basement as one which was in the Smalls' cottage, and spoke of Frederick and Florence's use of parlor matches on a regular basis. The mystery of the type of lock installed on the side door was further shattered by Norma's testimony. She recollected it was a self-locking latch, which made a strange clicking sound. To release the lock, pressure had to be exerted on a small button. This description of the lock seemed to correspond to similar testimony by Phillip Davis and George Kennett.

Norma's final testimony concerned Frederick Small's use of vulgar language when speaking about, and to, his wife. When Mr. Matthews, attorney for the defense, displayed several different kinds of knots to Norma Curry, she correctly selected the square knot she had witnessed Frederick Small tie on several occasions in the past.

Throughout the medical testimony, Frederick Small's uneasiness was well noted. However when Norma was testifying, the smile returned to Frederick's face, especially as she spoke of the vulgar language he directed toward his wife during Norma's brief stay with her sister in October. But Small grinned from ear to ear as Norma spoke of his proficiency in tying a square knot, since he was apparently proud of this accomplishment and was pleased to be receiving public recognition for his adeptness in this area. Throughout the period when the Curry women were testifying, the courtroom was overflowing with spectators. The air in the courtroom became so stuffy that a woman fainted and had to be removed during the testimony.

With these final witnesses on January 5, 1917, the prosecution rested its case. Judge Kivel must have been extremely anxious by now, since the anticipated Tuesday closing of the prosecution's case had turned into Friday. There appeared to have been even more urgency at this point for the trial to end. Ten days was an extended period of time for a prosecution to lay out its case, and the sequestered jury had to have wondered if this trial would ever end.

The Currys planned to remain in town for the duration of the trial, and were treated graciously by all they met. Of all attending the sensational proceedings, the Currys' feelings of betrayal had to have been insurmountable. For the man to whom the Currys entrusted Florence's life had beguiled them in the worst possible way. The picturesque scene of an early winter snow falling on the quaint streets of Ossipee, overlooking the snowcapped mountains of the region, had to have been breathtaking to all who were fortunate enough to witness the event. But one could only imagine the pain of Elizabeth and Norma Curry, as they watched the snow gently falling on the remaining pieces of Florence's former home, where her ashes still endured, frozen in the ice restrained by the walls of the remaining fieldstone foundation.

VIII. The Trial

[1] "Small Jury is Complete, Trial Now Under Way," *The Manchester Leader and Evening Union*, Dec. 27, 1916, pg. 2.

[2] Ibid., pg. 2.

[3] "Small's Trial Begins Today," *Manchester Union Leader*, Dec. 26, 1916, pg. 1.

[4] Woodbury, pg. 1.

[5] Ibid., pg. 1.

[6] Harkness and McGrew, pg. 92.

[7] Ibid., pg. 92.

[8] Ibid., pg. 92.

[9] "Small Jury is Complete, Trial Now Under Way," *The Manchester Leader and Evening Union*, Dec. 27, 1916, pg. 1.

[10] Harkness and McGrew, pg. 93.

[11] Ibid., pg. 93.

[12] "Small Had Made Threats," *Concord Evening Monitor*, Dec. 29, 1916, pg. 1.

[13] "Declares Small Had Threatened to Murder Wife," *The Manchester Leader and Evening Union*, Dec. 28, 1916, pg. 7.

[14] "Chase Describes Small's Interest in Joint Policy," *The Manchester Leader and Evening Union*, Dec. 29, 1916, pg. 2.

[15] Ibid., pg. 2.

[16] Ibid., pg. 2.

[17] "Small's Inventory Made No Mention of Jewelry," *The Manchester Leader and Evening Union*, Dec. 30, 1916, pg. 3.

[18] "Inventory Discussed, Revolver Identified," *Concord Evening Monitor*, Dec. 30, 1916, pg. 1.

[19] Harkness and McGrew, pg. 95.

[20] "Woman Was Strangled," *Concord Evening Monitor*, Concord, NH, Jan. 1, 1917, pg. 1.

[21] "Court Puts Ban on Contents of Laura's Letters," *The Manchester Leader and Evening Union*, Jan. 2, 1917, pg. 7.

[22] The State of New Hampshire Superior Court, *State vs. Frederick L. Small*, Carroll County Courthouse, December Term, 1916, pg. 4.

[23] "General Denial is Defense of Broker Small," *The Manchester Leader and Evening Union*, Jan. 5, 1917, pg. 12.

[24] The State of New Hampshire Superior Court, *State vs. Frederick L. Small*, Carroll County Courthouse, December Term, 1916, pg. 19.

IX. IN DEFENSE

As World War I raged on and U.S. submarines became increasingly more effective against their weakening enemies, Frederick Small's trial continued to captivate the local communities surrounding Ossipee. As a result of the ongoing trial, Judge Kivel and Attorney General Tuttle were unable to attend the governor's ball in Concord. This ball was proclaimed to have outshined all other balls preceding it, and was always a good opportunity for men in the political arena to enjoy an evening with colleagues. However, the opportunity for statewide notoriety presented itself on an even larger scale right in Ossipee, if the prosecution could secure a conviction and the judge could operate a just, yet expeditious, trial.

At this time, Frederick Small's defense team took over as they prepared to motion the court for an acquittal. A motion for acquittal was fairly common practice in this sort of case, and upon the possibility that the decision of the court was to deny this motion, the defense had to prepare itself to convince twelve men of their client's innocence, or at the very least, to create a reasonable doubt. Frederick Small would finally be granted the chance to defend himself. On his behalf, Sidney Stevens began to outline the defense strategy on January 5.

First, however, it was William Matthews' duty, as senior counsel for the defense, to motion for an acquittal, asserting that the state didn't provide sufficient evidence to further prosecute his client for this crime. Judge Kivel had predicted this request, and questioned the defense about why they felt an acquittal should be granted.

Matthews, who was characterized by James Welch as "an old trial lawyer who had won many cases in that court at Ossipee,"[1] contended the defense wasn't denying that Florence Small was murdered, only that the prosecution had charged the wrong man with the crime. The defense maintained that throughout the day and night of September 28, 1916, Frederick Small exhibited the behavior of any normal man. Surely if Frederick had committed the heinous act the prosecution depicted, he wouldn't have been able to act so naturally as he went about his day. With regard to Frederick's house and life insurance policies, folks would have thought him remiss not to have made provisions to care for his family in the event of some tragedy. Frederick was only performing the "duty which every man owes to his family."[2] The prosecution's claim that the murder occurred during the early afternoon of September 28 was contested by the defense, who proposed that Florence was murdered in the evening, immediately following a meal of warmed over stew or soup. The defense further asserted that the side door through which Frederick left that afternoon had been locked by Florence Small, who was still alive at the time; not by Frederick with the aid of a spring lock, as the prosecution had claimed. Furthermore, the defense indicated that Frederick Small never had possession of a vibratory coil, a crucial element in creating an incendiary device using a spark plug, which was listed by the prosecution as one of the ingredients of the fire-starting device. For that matter, there was no real evidence presented to prove that Frederick Small started a fire some seven hours after he left the cottage. Neither was there any evidence that Small had possession of thermit or that he even had knowledge of the very existence of the compound. As for the other articles found in the cottage ruins, the defense insisted that any given household in the area would commonly have similar items. And finally, although Frederick Small was known to be good with knots, there were many people in the Ossipee area capable of tying a neat square knot such as the one used to tie the cord which strangled Florence Small. With this submission of the defense's arguments for acquittal, the prosecution began to rebut the defense's claims.

Mr. Tuttle stood to oppose the motion for acquittal, stating that the poker, the revolver, and the cord that caused the death of Florence Small were all proven to have been owned by the defendant. The knot that was tied securing the cord around Mrs. Small's neck was an exact replica of knots that Small had tied in other instances. The state's final objection led to the recalling of Ed Connor as a witness for the prosecution. The state contended that during his trip to Boston, Small indicated that he had knowledge of the crime before he was told of it. Ed Connor testified that when the hotel had informed Small there was a phone call from Ossipee that fateful night, Frederick leaned over to Ed and said, "Come here, I want you to be sure and hear this."[3]

At the close of the prosecution's rebuttal, Judge Kivel didn't have to take a recess to ponder the opposing arguments for the acquittal of Frederick Small. After sitting in the courtroom and listening to the testimony presented thus far, Judge Kivel deemed there was, indeed, enough evidence to proceed with the trial of Frederick Small. The defense arguments had not swayed his opinion.

Consequently, the defense began their case, disclosing to the press that the trial would not be ending that week, since the defense planned to call fifteen to eighteen witnesses, not including Small himself. When reporters pressed for an answer as to whether Frederick Small would testify in his own defense, his attorneys replied that the decision had not been made yet. Estimates stood that the trial would last another three days, if Small wasn't called to testify.

The defense choose to begin by negating testimony concerning Small's handwritten inventory. Herbert W. Hobbs of Mountainview was called to the stand by Stevens to testify that in November 1915 he purchased a parlor heater from Frederick Small. Hobbs also noted that he had never heard Frederick use vulgar or abusive language around Florence. This testimony, however, was immediately disallowed by the judge and stricken from the record. Following Hobbs on the witness stand was Fred B. Foss, called to affirm that his company sold a heater to Frederick Small in November 1915. Foss was able to positively identify the stove recovered from the ruins of the cottage as being identical to the one his company sold to Small. As treasurer of the company, Foss had retained records indicating the precise price Small paid for the item. Through the testimony of these two witnesses, Stevens was able to prove the stove listed in the inventory was the old one sold to Hobbs, not the one that replaced it, which ultimately wound up in the cottage rubble after the fire. Thus, Stevens had proven the inventory found in Frederick's satchel was old, and hadn't been hurriedly written the day of the murder, as the prosecution contended.

As it became more evident that Small would not take the stand in his own defense, his lawyers continued on Saturday, January 6, to make their case. Mr. Stevens called Arthur W. Brunt to the stand, who told of witnessing the recovery of the old-fashioned lock near the side door of the cottage. According to Brunt, the bolt was found in a locked position with the key still attached to the inside, confirming the statements of several other witnesses. Stevens asserted that this evidence should sufficiently serve to prove the door was locked by Florence Small from the inside after Frederick's departure from the cottage.

Then, Stevens called Sheriff Chandler and Dr. Hodsdon to the stand, two witnesses who firmly favored a conviction for Small. Stevens asked both men of the circumstances in which the lock had reached their hands, as a means of presenting the lock to the jury. But reports of the lock exchanging hands many times, with Chandler himself seeing the key turned at least two times in his presence, reduced the reliability of previous testimony of whether the door was locked or unlocked following Small's departure from the cottage.

The defense immediately countered by calling several newspapermen to the stand who were on the scene at the time the lock was discovered. John Casey, Roy Atkinson, and Charles Merrill were questioned by the defense, then cross-examined by Tuttle. John Casey was the primary witness concerning the lock, since he was the one who turned it over to the authorities. Casey stated the lock was located in the area where the side door had stood, frozen with the bolt out. Casey spoke of handing the lock to the sheriff, who in turn, handed it to Prosecutor Hill. However, under cross-examination Casey admitted he didn't know what door the lock had come from, and he wasn't sure that he was the first person to pick the lock up from the ground. Casey admitted that someone else could have picked up the lock from another area of the property and discarded it in the place where he ultimately found it. Casey also revealed that one of the men he gave the lock to turned the key once, and he didn't know if the key was turned from the inside or the outside. In conclusion, Casey agreed the lock could have been from any door in the house, as there was no door sill near the lock to give a clue of its former location.

The defense quickly followed this line of testimony with an additional witness, the Smalls' butcher, who often delivered meat to the cottage. George F. Tasker spoke of Frederick Small as being an excellent host, often offering him whiskey or brandy when he dropped by with the couple's order. Tasker was also present at the time the lock was located in the rubble, having accidently kicked it while walking through some of the debris from the fire. Tasker picked up the lock and handed it to Casey. Tasker thought the key was turned from the inside of the lock. But testimony from George Huckins, a lumber dealer from Freedom who was also present when the lock was found, varied from Tasker's. He couldn't tell whether the key was turned from the inside or the outside, and wasn't even certain the lock on exhibit was the lock he had seen that day. Huckins was astounded when he was called to the witness stand, clearly not expecting to be called to testify.

To further indicate the type of locks used in the Smalls' house, Frank L. Harriman, the carpenter who built the Small cottage, was called to the stand. Harriman verified that he installed only one night lock, which was located on the front door. But the prosecution found a serious flaw in this testimony, recalling that the side addition was not built when the original home was constructed. Therefore, Harriman would have no knowledge concerning the lock that was installed on the side door. With that, Harriman was dismissed from the witness stand.

Following Harriman's testimony, Leonard Blizzard was called to the stand. Blizzard was the bellboy on duty at Young's Hotel, where Ed Connor and Frederick Small stayed in Boston on September 28. Blizzard spoke of tears flowing down Frederick's cheeks as he waited on the sidewalk for the car they hired to return to Ossipee.

Next, the defense attempted to demonstrate that the wire found in the rubble of the cottage was part of the telephone wiring installed in the home, rather than part of an incendiary device. To illustrate this point, Mr. Stevens called John Rancy of North Conway to the stand. Rancy described rerouting a substantial amount of telephone wiring in the Smalls' cottage in 1914. Rancy was able to give a clear description of the location of these additional wires in the cottage. The defense had to have been pleased with Rancy as a witness as they sat down to allow the prosecution's cross-examination. However, with the prosecution unable to dispute Rancy's testimony, Tuttle strayed to a loosely connected subject when he asked Rancy if batteries commonly used in telephone service could be converted to successfully function in an incendiary device. Rancy thought for a moment, before answering that those types of batteries could be used for such a purpose.

Immediately following Rancy's testimony, the defense began a lengthy list of character witnesses. First on the stand was Mr. William A. Gould of Southborough, Massachusetts, who worked as a highway surveyor and knew Small when he resided in Southborough. Gould gave a glowing report of Small's character. Yet upon cross-examination, when Gould was asked questions concerning the fire which destroyed the Curry homestead, Gould stated that he knew little about the fire. Following Gould to the witness stand were two local painters who had worked at the Smalls' cottage. Charles Ross and Fred Johnson testified they never heard Frederick speak abusively to his wife. As a matter of fact, neither man ever heard the couple disagree while they worked on the Smalls' property. Nathaniel Mitchell, Frederick's nephew, was called to the stand to verify that he, too, had never heard a profane word or abusive language used by his uncle when visiting with the Smalls. And finally, Minor L. Small was called to the stand to affirm that the motor in the Smalls' boat didn't use spark plugs similar to those found by the investigators in the cottage.

The most surprising testimony of the day was Dr. Lindsey Grant's of Somersworth. Upon examination, Grant noted a thin, red line located just between the burned and unburned portions of Florence's body. According to Grant, this line was a sign that Mrs. Small was alive at the time of the burning, or had just been killed prior to being set on fire. Grant's reasoning was that if rigor mortis had already set in before the burning, this line wouldn't have appeared on Florence's body. Collaborating Grant's statement was the testimony of Dr. Harry Anderson of Milton Mills, Maine, who followed Grant to the witness stand. Dr. Anderson further stated that the substance found on Mrs. Small's body appeared to possess all of the characteristics of glass, rather than resin as the prosecution maintained. Dr. William E. Elliott of Berwick, Maine, also backed up Dr. Grant and Dr. Anderson with similar testimony regarding the narrow red line, "the line of demarcation."[4] If these three doctors were correct in their theory, Frederick Small couldn't possibly have killed Florence. Small had an airtight alibi from 3 o'clock in the afternoon until the time of the fire, shortly before 10 o'clock that night. If evidence proved that Florence was killed just prior to the fire, then Frederick Small had to be exonerated and set free. The only question remaining—would the jury of twelve men believe the testimony of these three doctors?

As the trial adjourned for the evening, as well as for the week, it seemed the end wouldn't draw near until Tuesday, at the very earliest. Furthermore, it now appeared the defense would not be calling Frederick Small to testify, even though his lawyers had suggested that Small's voice would eventually be heard, substantiating his innocence. Although the inclusion of Small's testimony had been considered highly probable and was anticipated by both spectators and officials to be the highlight of the trial, the defense team opted to forego their client's affirmation, stating that after scrutinizing the prosecution's case, they were confident this testimony was not necessary to vindicate their client. However, the prosecution's seventy-seven exhibits were far from matched by the defense's plan to introduce nine additional items to the court. Among these exhibits was a scaled-down model of a door resembling the side door of the Smalls' cottage for the jury to examine.

On January 8, 1917, final arguments were presented in the case of The State vs. Frederick L. Small. People flocked to the little town of Ossipee using any mode of transportation available to them, be it train, automobile or sleigh. Entire families came into town, armed with boxed lunches to assure they wouldn't lose their seating during the noon recess. Every seat in the courtroom was taken, and the corridors were filled as well. Those outside the courtroom huddled around telegraph wires in the basement of the courthouse, or gathered together on icy sidewalks beneath courtroom windows. It was predicted that by midnight, Small's fate would be sealed.

As court resumed, the defense presented a motion that the court instruct the jury to hand down a decision of not guilty, as the state did not present sufficient evidence to commission the jury to decide the case. This motion was promptly denied by Judge Kivel. With the defense's last hopes of avoiding jury deliberations slashed, Mr. Matthews rose from his chair, to begin his closing arguments on Frederick Small's behalf. Matthews first clarified for the jury that in order to find Frederick Small responsible for this crime the prosecution must have proven him guilty beyond a reasonable doubt. Mr. Matthews then reminded the jury that every piece of evidence the prosecution presented was entirely circumstantial. Circumstantial evidence, Matthews asserted, must be proven before it can be considered. There wasn't a shred of direct evidence to link their client to the crime.

Mr. Matthews then proceeded to discount the prosecution's allegations. "To put the insurance policy as a motive in this case is to turn into a motive that which is a man's duty toward his family,"[5] Matthews maintained. Furthermore, Matthews affirmed that Small presented no indication that anything out of the ordinary had occurred the afternoon of September 28, referring to Small's unaffected handwriting on a check used to record business mileage from Ossipee to Boston, shortly after the prosecution alleged the murder had taken place. Then Matthews asked the jury to consider what man would have chosen to attend the performance of a tragic show that evening in Boston, if he had just murdered his wife and set his home on fire? Matthews further alleged that Frederick Small's complete change in demeanor after receiving the phone call concerning the fire and the possible death of his wife proved that he had no previous knowledge of the event.

The defense continued to attack the prosecution's evidence by pointing out that Small's intent was to open a safe deposit box in Boston to store his sentimental keepsakes and important papers, all of which he had brought with him on his trip to Boston. Furthermore, Dr. Kingsford's testimony that Florence was killed right after eating a hearty meal at noon was considered speculative, since there were no witnesses to the meal except for Frederick himself. The defense contended the meat and vegetables consumed by Florence shortly before the murder indicated an evening meal of warmed-over soup. Dr. Kingsford's discovery of resin covering the body of Florence Small was also disputed, when the defense reminded the jury that expert witnesses had determined the substance to be that of glass. The final item in this laundry list of evidence was the allegation of abusive treatment of Florence Small by her husband. The defense attorneys' estimation of this component of the prosecution's case was, at best, weak.

To add some irony to the case, Matthews loudly declared, "Do you suppose a man who would attempt to carry through such a premeditated crime would allow suspicion to attach itself to him, by buying kerosene at the last minute?" [6] Surely if this crime had been premeditated to the degree that an incendiary device had been researched, assembled, and tested, as the prosecution insisted, the murderer would have made certain the required amount of kerosene had been stored away in the cottage to assure its availability and divert suspicion. This topic served Mr. Matthews with a convenient transition to the incendiary device; where the defense insisted the spark plug found in the ruins had a serious defect in it, which would have interfered with the ability of the device to work. Even witnesses for the prosecution had agreed with this point. And the clockworks that were supposedly used in assembling this presumed incendiary device had been missing for years.

Mr. Matthews continued the defense's summation by stating that Florence was alive when Frederick left for Boston, that Frederick said good-bye to her, and that George Kennett wasn't certain if he had heard a lock click. But when the lock was discovered, the key was on the inside of the lock. "I don't think you'll have any difficulty in finding that the click Kennett heard was the turning of this lock at the hand of Mrs. Small,"[7] Matthews contended.

Finally, the defense explained that the red line of demarcation that existed between the burned and unburned parts of Mrs. Small's body, proved that she wasn't quite dead or had just died nearing the time of the fire. Matthews summarized for the jury that if the fire happened close to 10:00 P.M., and Frederick had left at 3:00 that afternoon, how could Frederick Small have been responsible for his wife's death?

In a final statement, Matthews announced to the court, "In closing, it was gratifying that the state had not made out such a case that it was necessary to put Frederick Small on the witness stand to refute it."[8] With that final remark, Matthews confidently took his seat beside his client. A recess was taken at the conclusion of the defense's closing statement.

With closing remarks of the defense behind them, James Welch, as well as the other eleven men chosen to serve on the jury, must have been relieved to see the trial coming to an end. Of Matthew's concluding statement, Welch later commented, "Will Matthew's final plea for the respondent was as good as any I ever heard. When he finished, men and women were crying. But though all the jurors liked Matthews, they paid little or no attention to his plea."[9]

Court resumed at 2:00 P.M., at which time the state, with Attorney General Tuttle as public orator, produced a quick rebuttal, refuting the presence of a red line on the burned body of Mrs. Small. Other topics mentioned by the prosecution consisted of a statement from Lilla Ferrin claiming the side door did, in fact, have a spring lock. Tuttle also presented the existence of a statement which proved documented, physical spousal abuse by the doctor who treated Florence Small in Southborough, even though this line of questioning wasn't permitted when Dr. Bacon previously testified for the prosecution. Tuttle's summation consisted of statements such as, "The motive is what Satan teaches his imps and disciples to do, and you get the circumstantial evidence of it from what the imp of Satan does."[10] Tuttle referred to their efforts in this trial as, "Not only have we had to meet the ability of able counsel but we have had to meet the devilish cunning and the hellish ingenuity of that disciple of Satan who is named in this indictment, and who sits before you where you have had a chance to see him and to know, in part, at least, what manner of man he is . . . . this masterful, mysterious, bloody man."[11]

Jurors heard the crime referred to as, "almost beyond the power of language to describe . . . ."[12] and the accused as, "the devilish cunning of a disciple of Satan."[13] Tuttle scoffed at the idea that someone may have entered the cottage through a basement window, collecting everything needed to commit the murder and set the fire. Tuttle proclaimed, "Tell me, Gentlemen, who else on earth had any interest to absolutely destroy the identity of that body except this respondent, in order that the bullet wound, the poker blows, the strangle cord, might go up in smoke?"[14] In referring to Small's state of mind on the evening of September 28 while he was in Boston, Tuttle extended the correlation, "Nero fiddled while Rome burned. Small ate scallops and drank Pickwick ale while his cottage burned. Frederick L. Small could give Nero points."[15] After refuting the medical testimony and the clicking of the door lock at the hand of Mrs. Small, Tuttle summarized his description of Small as, "sometimes masterful, sometimes emotional, but always in perfect control."[16]

Both sides had finished their closing statements by 4:30 that afternoon, leaving Tuttle to give an impassioned plea to the jury to find for murder in the first degree, with the inclusion of capital punishment because, as Tuttle put it, "This was the most brutal crime in New Hampshire since the days of Indian massacres."[17] With that, he dangled the blood-stained cord, which had once encircled Florence Small's neck, in front of Frederick Small, and then, in turn, before each one of the juror's eyes. Following the closing statements, the defense rose to object to many of the innuendoes Tuttle used to describe Small. Tuttle graciously agreed to withdraw many of these inflammatory remarks from the court record, knowing full well his harsh words would not soon be forgotten, ringing in the jurymen's ears for some time to come.

Throughout closing statements, Small sat in his usual stoic manner, his eyes bound to the jurymen's faces. Newspapermen, who anxiously listened to both sides, knowing they would need to submit competitively detailed reports of the summations, abbreviated their impressions of the closing arguments. One reporter wrote of closing statements, "In rhetorical flights the argument of the prosecution was alive with thrills, while that of the defense was more quiet, but still frequent with possibilities."[18]

Insight into the jury's feeling for the prosecution's case was later summarized by Welch, "The evidence was all circumstantial, but the jurors thought the circumstances were so positive that they fitted together and made a chain better than direct evidence."[19] Welch also reflected the jury's belief that the witnesses for the defense weren't "the same high type"[20] as the prosecution's witnesses.

At 5:42 P.M., Judge Kivel began his summary of the law as it applied to this trial, and by 6:22 that evening, the case was delivered to the jury. At 7:55 P.M., after a break for dinner, the jury began deliberations in the courthouse, with three possible decisions from which to choose. For the prosecution, the jury could make one of two choices: guilty of first degree murder with the recommendation for capital punishment, or guilty of murder in the first degree with a recommendation of life imprisonment. For the defense, the jury had only one option available to them: acquittal.

For the most part, during closing statements Small sat quietly. However there was one point when attorneys for both sides found it necessary to meet with Judge Kivel at the bench. Small took part in this conference, standing elbow to elbow with the judge, frowning. Nevertheless, by the time Small had left the conference, the frown had disappeared. As Small left the courthouse, he smiled at the newspaper reporters and lit up a cigar. When asked how he felt, Small grinned and said, "I feel fine and also confident."[21]

James Welch later summed up the sentiment of the jury as they met to deliberate as, "feeling sorry for Will Matthews. It was a shame to waste such good legal talent on a man like Small."[22] Welch also noted, "I think that when the jury retired for deliberation every man on that panel felt in his own mind that Judge Kivel thought that Small was guilty and should hang."[23] However the local newspaper which served the Ossipee area printed of the trial, "If ever a trial was conducted with more fairness to both state and respondent, or a Judge's charge to the jury more impartially delivered than was Judge Kivel's we fail to recall."[24]

While the jury was meeting, it seemed that everyone who was even remotely connected to the Small trial retired to the Carroll Inn at dinnertime. As one New Hampshire newspaper dramatically put it, "All the actors in the Ossipee murder mystery were under the same roof at the Carroll Inn at the meal hour."[25] Judge Kivel and the prosecutors dined at a corner table, while Mrs. Curry and her daughter, and Small's attorneys sat at nearby tables. Newspaper reporters, spectators, and witnesses filled the rest of the dining room. It was a credit to the participants of this trial that all these different factions could occupy the same close space without any kind of conflict arising. Frederick Small was in an upstairs room at the Carroll Inn, eating a substantial meal, his appetite apparently unaffected by the tension of the evening. Following his dinner, Frederick sat in a comfortable chair, shedding his suitcoat and smoking his usual cigar in the company of George Philbrick, the deputy sheriff. The jurymen were in yet another area of the rambling inn, enjoying their dinner as best they could, with the daunting task awaiting them at the conclusion of their meal.

Before dinner, newspaper reporters had been busy doing some last minute editorializing for their evening papers. *The Manchester Leader and Evening Union* speculated, "If the state has proved its case, it has developed a new type of New Hampshire criminal. It has brought forth a cool, daring, mechanical and chemical genius, a man who scorned the ordinary forms of murder but who brought to the mountains of this quiet village a science which would baffle a Craig Kennedy or Sherlock Holmes. The jury of his peers will decide whether Frederick L. Small is that man or the normal individual who has been made a victim of circumstances and is being tried for a crime which he never committed and of which he had no knowledge."[26] This was quite a legacy for Frederick Small, who back as a little boy in Portland, Maine, had always dreamed of fame and fortune, 'though on the baseball field.

Small walked back to the courthouse at around 8:00 in the evening to await his verdict. The closer Small came to the courthouse, the more cheerful he became, convinced that in just a few short hours, he would be a free man. He was especially encouraged when Mrs. Marsh, the court stenographer, made the announcement that the notes from the trial were so lengthy they filled thirteen separate volumes. Small had always been convinced that thirteen was his lucky number. The final two digits on his revolver allegedly used in the murder were thirteen. Likewise, the $20,000 life insurance policy that played a key role in the trial was purchased on March 13, 1916. Adding to this bazaar coincidence, the number on the door of Small's room at Young's Hotel in Boston that fateful night of the fire was 113. In a few short hours, which would seem like an eternity to everyone involved with the trial, Frederick Small would discover if thirteen truly was his good luck charm.

It was shortly before 11:00 P.M. when word buzzed around the Carroll County Courthouse that the verdict was in. Most everybody had stayed in town that night, since many felt a verdict was near. Most everybody, that is, with the exception of nearly all the women who had, up until now, shared an interest in the trial. That evening, however, there were only four women in attendance to hear the verdict. As everyone crowded into the dimly lit courtroom once more, Frederick Small was escorted to his seat, which was set into place by his brother. Small had been waiting for word of the verdict in the courthouse library with the deputy sheriff. Soon after, the jury returned to their seats, followed by Judge Kivel. The defense council and Frederick Small rose for the reading of the verdict at precisely 11:13 P.M. Although the courtroom was filled with spectators, a pin drop could have been heard, as anticipation of the verdict reached its peak. It was the court clerk's responsibility to question the jury.

Arthur E. Kenison rose and formally asked, "Gentlemen of the jury, are you agreed upon a verdict?"[27]

Foreman Elmer N. Berry responded for the jury by saying, "We have."[28]

Kenison replied by asking, "What say you? Is the prisoner at the bar guilty of the crime of which he here stands charged, or not guilty?"[29]

Elmer Berry hesitated slightly before stating, "Guilty of murder in the first degree, with capital punishment."[30]

The courtroom remained eerily silent. After an initial cringing motion, Frederick Small stood expressionless, almost as though the verdict was one that held meaning for a man other than himself. Small's eyes teared slightly, but blinking the tears away, Small looked at the jury evenly. The last hanging that had occurred in the state of New Hampshire was thought to have already taken place, with the hanging of convicted murderer Comery. Although most people following the Small trial were anticipating a guilty verdict, even the most fervent of those had not foreseen the inclusion of capital punishment in the murderer's sentence. Court was adjourned until 9:00 the next morning, at which time sentencing was to be passed down. The jury was dismissed for the night, and Frederick Small shook hands with many of the newspaper reporters, "thanking them for their courtesy and their kindness."[31]

Small turned to his brother as he buttoned up his overcoat saying, "I'll see you in the morning, Frank."[32] Then he shook hands with his nephew, who was also present for the verdict.

As he was escorted back to jail for the night, Small told those reporters who continued to follow him, "I am prepared for the next move. Gentlemen, I am as innocent of the crime as you are."[33]

Likewise, Small's counsel added, "We will perfect our appeal tomorrow. We have taken many exceptions and believe some of them are good ones. We are confident of the ultimate results."[34] From outward appearances, Small's attorneys had been far more shaken by the verdict than Frederick Small himself.

On the way to the county jailhouse, Small lit up the stub of a cigar, with a noticeable tremble in his hand. Then Matthews whispered an inaudible comment into Small's ear, to which Small responded in a somewhat strained tone of voice, "I have no feelings against anyone."[35]

When asked to respond to the verdict passed down by the jury that night, Attorney General Tuttle was quoted as saying simply, "It is a just verdict."[36]

Following the adjournment of court proceedings for the night, many members of the jury were seen greeting spectators with smiles and jubilation. They must have been relieved to finally have been released from their burden of sequestered jury duty. Newspapermen reported the jury's state of mind as being one of gladness, and felt the jurors "were in the mood of a hard task well done."[37] When reporters queried some of the jurors as to how many ballots were taken in reaching the final verdict, jurymen chose not to comment. It seems the jurors had already agreed amongst themselves not to devulge that kind of information, thus no one was able to secure the particulars of the deliberations at that time. It wasn't until about twenty-five years later when one of the jurymen and farmers, James Welch, who eventually became sheriff of Carroll County himself, would write a book in which one chapter revealed the jury's state of mind during the trial, summation, and deliberations.

In an effort to summarize the entire experience, James Welch wrote, "This was my first murder trial, and the ugliness of it is still with me. I was glad when those fifteen days were over and I could get out into the woods and fields again. I have never been able to understand why a man with money and an education should commit a crime that such families as they call decadent, up there behind the Ossipees, could never even think of."[38]

Oddly enough, Florence's mother and sister had retired for the evening and had not heard the verdict. It wasn't until they were seated in the dining room for breakfast that a newspaper reporter approached them for their reaction to the verdict. When learning of the verdict for the first time, Mrs. Curry accepted it in the calm, maternal manner in which she had conducted herself throughout the course of the trial. However, Norma Curry began to collapse as the verdict took on meaning for her. Several townspeople rushed to her aid and in a few minutes she was feeling more herself.

When pressed for a statement, Mrs. Curry replied, "The verdict is a just one. If there ever was an incarnate fiend on earth he is one. If people could know what we were not permitted to tell in court they would know why we feel as we do."[39]

Norma Curry followed her mother's reply with these few words of vindication, "For once justice overtook him."[40]

At 9:21, on the morning of January 9, Judge Kivel entered the courtroom. Frederick Small and counsel for the defense as well as the prosecution were in attendance. But notably, the majority of the crowds had vanished. There was a grand, mass departure from the little town of Ossipee, which began early that morning, leaving the village feeling much like a ghost town.

"I have considered the motion for sentence made last night by the county solicitor," Judge Kivel began, "Frederick L. Small, have you anything to say, why sentence of death should not be passed upon you at this time?"[41]

At that moment, Small began to limp towards the bench, quietly stating, "I have, your honor."[42]

"Stay where you are,"[43] Judge Kivel stated firmly, as he raised his hand toward Small.

Small immediately stopped in his tracks. Then, raising his eyes to meet Judge Kivel's stern stare squarely, Small stated in a deep, nasal toned voice, "I know no more about this crime than you do. I am an innocent person."[44]

Judge Kivel then proceeded to ask the court clerk, Arthur Kenison, to read the sentencing. Kenison began by stating that Small would be incarcerated in the Concord State Prison until January 15, 1918, at which time he would be executed for his crime. Then, he concluded with the chilling words, "It is the sentence of this court that you shall be hanged by the neck, until you are dead."[45]

This statement appeared to have as minute an effect on Frederick Small as the reading of the verdict the night before. In concluding the sentencing, Judge Kivel offered Small the option of ten days in which he and his counsel could file any exceptions to the trial. The judge also made it known that if they were to need an extension of this time frame, the extension would be granted. The sentencing only lasted three minutes, at which time Small was led out of the courtroom and back to the custody of the Carroll County jailhouse. Sheriff Chandler escorted the prisoner to jail, at which time all of his possessions were taken from him. Subsequently, Small was placed on round-the-clock supervision to prevent any suicide attempt to foil the state's ability to carry out the sentence of capital punishment. This duty of surveillance fell into the hands of the sheriff's deputy, George Philbrick. In a few days, Small would be transferred to the state prison in Concord, New Hampshire, where he would be allowed to prepare any final efforts to regain his life.

In a strange twist of fate, Mr. Matthews, counsel for the defense, announced his intention to immediately begin an investigation into the death of Dr. Sarah A. Jenness from the neighboring town of Wolfeboro, who was found burned to death in her home on December 26, 1916. According to Matthews, this case and the case of the murder of Florence Arlene Curry Small had many similarities, and could possibly have been linked.

However, upon careful examination of the death of Sarah Jenness, similarities seemed to fall apart. Sarah Jenness died in the home in which she was born, in a tragic fire. She began her career as a school teacher, having graduated from Abbott Academy in Andover, Massachusetts, and moved down South to teach for a while, before returning to Boston to earn her medical degree. Dr. Jenness practiced medicine for a number of years, until a stroke and poor health caused her to retire to her family's farm in New Hampshire. Dr. Jenness loved books and poetry, and especially the old farm house, where she lived alone. Having just been brought some food and firewood from some helpful neighbors the morning of the fire, the well-loved Dr. Jenness was thought to have sustained another stroke, since she had suffered two additional strokes since moving home. It was theorized that during this spell, Dr. Jenness had somehow set her house on fire, burning it to the ground. An autopsy showed no sign of foul play. Dr. Jenness died at the age of seventy-four. The only similarities between Florence Small's and Dr. Jenness' cases were that they both died in a fire, and were alone at the time the fire broke out. Mr. Matthews wasn't going to convince a judge to overturn the verdict with examination of the similarities in these two cases.

On January 10, 1917, Frederick Small was transported to prison in Concord, New Hampshire, to work on his appeal, or possibly, to await his execution. In the company of Sheriff Chandler and two deputies, Small occupied the next to last car of the Central Vermont Express, as it rolled into the Manchester station for a brief stopover. Observers noted that Small, who occupied a window seat, was smoking his usual black cigar and peering out at the spectators who came to catch a glimpse of the infamous murderer. Small appeared to be comfortably parleying with his attendants, as he puffed on his cigar, undisturbed by the crowd which had gathered. Small's journey required two changes of trains, one in Rochester, and the second in Nashua, before arriving at his destination, a cell in the Concord State Prison. A taxi was waiting at the Concord train station to transport Frederick Small to the institution. As he entered the prison walls, Small was unusually silent, and observers wondered if he finally grasped the meaning of his sentence. The warden, Charles H. Rowe, took custody of the prisoner, who freely answered the warden's questions. Small was given his change of clothing and was assigned to a cell. Barring successful appeal, this would be where Small would spend the duration of his life, and this train ride would certainly have been his last journey. This was a far cry from the peaceful setting of Small's residence of the past three years, where the picturesque shores of Lake Ossipee had provided a panoramic view, and a fieldstone foundation which would probably haunt him for the duration of his existence.

[1] Harkness and McGrew, pg. 93.
[2] "General Denial is Defense of Broker Small," *The Manchester Leader and Evening Union*, Jan. 5, 1917, pg. 12.
[3] Ibid., pg. 12.
[4] "Locked on the Inside," *Concord Evening Monitor*, Jan. 6, 1917, pg. 1.
[5] "Arguments Presented," *Concord Evening Monitor*, Jan. 8, 1917, pg. 1.

[6] Ibid., pg. 1.

[7] Ibid., pg. 3.

[8] Ibid., pg. 3.

[9] Harkness and McGrew, pg. 95.

[10] The State of New Hampshire Superior Court, *State vs. Frederick Small: Respondent's Bill of Exceptions*, Carroll County Courthouse, December Term, 1916, pg. 19.

[11] Ibid., pg. 19.

[12] "Arguments Presented," *Concord Evening Monitor*, Jan. 8, 1917, pg. 3.

[13] Ibid., pg. 3.

[14] The State of New Hampshire Superior Court, *State vs. Frederick Small: Respondent's Bill of Exceptions*, Carroll County Courthouse, December Term, 1916, pg. 19.

[15] "'I am Innocent' Prisoner Cries Before Sentence," *The Manchester Leader and Evening Union*, Jan. 9, 1917, pg. 9.

[16] "Arguments Presented," *Concord Evening Monitor*, Jan. 8, 1917, pg. 3.

[17] "'I am Innocent' Prisoner Cries Before Sentence," *The Manchester Leader and Evening Union*, Jan. 9, 1917, pg. 9.

[18] Ibid., pg. 9.

[19] Harkness and McGrew, pg. 95.

[20] Ibid., pg. 95.

[21] "Final Arguments in Small Murder Trial Are Begun," *The Manchester Leader and Evening Union*, Jan. 8, 1917, pg. 3.

[22] Harkness and McGrew, pg. 95.

[23] Ibid., pg. 95.

[24] "Small Case," *The Granite State News*, Jan. 13, 1917, pg. 1.

[25] "'I am Innocent' Prisoner Cries Before Sentence," *The Manchester Leader and Evening Union*, Jan. 9, 1917, pg. 9.

[26] "Final Arguments in Small Murder Trial Are Begun," *The Manchester Leader and Evening Union*, Jan. 8, 1917, pg. 3.

[27] "'I am Innocent' Prisoner Cries Before Sentence," *The Manchester Leader and Evening Union*, Jan. 9, 1917, pg. 9.

[28] Ibid., pg. 9.

[29] Ibid., pg. 9.

[30] Ibid., pg. 9.

[31] Ibid., pg. 9.

[32] Ibid., pg. 9.

[33] Ibid., pg. 9.

[34] Ibid., pg. 9.

[35] Ibid., pg. 9.

[36] Ibid., pg. 9.

[37] Ibid., pg. 9.

[38] Harkness and McGrew, pg. 96.

[39] "'I am Innocent' Prisoner Cries Before Sentence," *The Manchester Leader and Evening Union*, Jan. 9, 1917, pg. 9.

[40] Ibid., pg. 9.

[41] Ibid., pg. 1.

[42] Ibid., pg. 1.

[43] Ibid., pg. 1.

[44] Ibid., pg. 1.

[45] Ibid., pg. 1.

x. QUESTIONS AND RESOLUTIONS

With Frederick Small tucked safely away at the Concord State Prison, the bustling town of Ossipee returned to being a sleepy, winter village. The crowds had gone home and newspaper reporters were no longer interested in the comings and goings of townspeople. Had it been summer, the change wouldn't have been as noticeable. But in the winter, with inclement weather and freezing temperatures, the town of Ossipee wasn't as active and there wasn't a lot to occupy folks' time and thoughts.

The promise of a sequel to the trial in the form of a presentation by Small's defense lawyers of their exceptions to the proceedings, although not nearly as exciting as the trial itself, offered a glimmer of hope for a little diversion in the remainder of winter 1917. Small's defense lawyers kept their word to draw up a long list of exceptions to much of the testimony from the trial. One of their primary focuses concerned the testimony given by state expert witnesses regarding the incendiary device that Small was presumed to have concocted in his workshop. The defense, for the most part, objected to all this testimony because no foundation had been laid by the state to show that the articles found in the cellar were connected in a manner that would have resulted in a fire for criminal purposes, as the prosecution claimed. The defense insisted that all of these items could be commonly found in most households in the area, where they were being used for legitimate purposes. There was no proof that these items, such as the wire, the dry cells, and the spark plug were used in any unlawful manner. This expert testimony was considered by the defense to be speculative, confusing to the jury, and prejudicial to their client.

The second exception stated by the defense regarded the exhibition of Florence Small's head, which was displayed for the jury. During the trial, the court found that this presentation was necessary in proving the trauma inflicted on it. On the same note, the defense took exception to Dr. George Donovan's testimony, when the prosecution attempted to establish the temperature that a wood fire would burn. The defense maintained this would depend on any number of things, such as the amount of timber in the building, the location of the origin of the fire, and what the ground was like where the fire burned. The defense concluded that no one could answer this question with any degree of accuracy. The court, on the other hand, felt this was evidence relevant to the case, and it was the jury's decision as to how much weight to give the answer.

The defense continued its exceptions by citing that all testimony concerning thermit should have been excluded. This was because there was no evidence that Frederick Small had possessed thermit, or even had knowledge of the chemical's existence. They also opposed the admission of some bundles of wire and a bed spring found in the cellar of the Small cottage, but again, the court deemed the jury had the right to see and hear about all of this evidence, giving it whatever weight they felt it deserved.

Finally, there were a number of phrases the prosecution used in their arguments to which the defense took exception. Some of these phrases, especially the ones concerning descriptions of the defendant, were considered by the defense discriminatory towards their client. The prosecution was responsible for many notable quotes, for which Mr. Tuttle could take full credit, including, "we have had to meet the devilish cunning and the hellish ingenuity of that disciple of Satan who is named in this indictment and who sits before you,"[1] and, "the motive is what Satan teaches his imps and disciples to do, and you get the circumstantial evidence of it from what the imp of Satan does."[2] Closing arguments contained many prejudicial phrases such as, "Mind you, Gentlemen, keep your eye on this gentleman, this imp of Satan that sits here who is named in the indictment."[3] And no one in the courtroom could ever have forgotten Tuttle's plea to the jury, which smacked of touches of patriotism and religion, and a hint of peer pressure,

"And I trust that you will soon arrive at a right conclusion, and that conclusion will be such that as the word goes across from hill to hill and from home to home across the State that the people of New Hampshire, and especially the people of the County of Carroll will feel that they can say, as of olden time, 'God reigns. Justice has been done. All is well with the world.'"[4] The prosecution had surely predicted the negative effect their rhetoric would have on the defendant's integrity, when consistently proposing a connection between Small and Satan, to a jury made up primarily of farmers and woodsmen. Although Tuttle withdrew many of these remarks at the end of the trial, he had made these references often enough to have produced a lasting impact.

Tuttle was also responsible for statements that misrepresented the facts of the case. "In the beginning they were trying to hint at suicide. Today, they admit the crime."[5] Tuttle knew well the defendant had pled innocent to the crime, yet he took the fact that the defense agreed a crime had been committed to a more general interpretation leading to a presumed admission of guilt by the defendant. Small's attorneys also took exception to their client being described as, "this man whose hands can do anything."[6] This remark had been entered into record only to demonstrate Small's mechanical ability, and was not intended to be taken in the broad context in which Tuttle was now using it. Although Judge Kivel attempted to qualify these and other remarks by instructing the jury with this general statement, "Whenever counsel have misstated evidence, you should lay it out of your minds; pay no attention to it; consider it as if it had not been said, and rely solely upon your own recollection of the evidence as it came from the mouths of witnesses,"[7] it is hard to believe that jurors were actually able to accomplish this. Human nature is such that when instructed to "pay no attention to that man behind the curtain,"[8] that is the first thing people seek out and remember best.

Although the Bill of Exceptions was, for the most part, allowed to be used if and when the defense argued its case before the Supreme Court, it was to no avail. On December 26, 1917, the New Hampshire Supreme Court refused to accept the defense's pleas for a new trial. It appeared that Frederick Small would have to face his day of execution on January 15, 1918.

But a glimmer of hope emerged on March 21, 1917, when Small became aware of a bill concerning the abolition of the capital punishment clause being formally debated and voted upon in the New Hampshire Legislature. This bill, which Representative Winant of Concord had previously introduced to the State House of Representatives while Small's trial was underway, was expected to warrant only a brief debate before being voted up or down that very day. In Winant's opening remarks, he stated, "capital punishment is fundamentally wrong if I read my Bible aright. It degrades the hangmen obliged to carry out the law and the method of drawing the juries under the present law leads the jurors to believe they are dutybound to bring in a death penalty."[9] Winant also made the point, using transcripts from the Peaslee murder trial, that a great many jurors must be dismissed from serving on a murder trial because they wouldn't vote for capital punishment under any circumstances. This, Winant insisted, narrows the range of jurors a defendant has available to hear his case. In conclusion, Winant defined capital punishment as "murder by judicial process."[10]

Following Winant's statement, Representative Nelson of Manchester agreed with Winant, stating there was no real necessity for the death penalty to continue on the books. Nelson cited that in 300 years of New Hampshire history, only twenty-one men had been executed for their crimes. With Winant's bill seconded by Mr. Nelson and Mr. Ahern of Concord, it seemed the measure might have actually had a chance to pass.

However, there was a good deal of opposition to the newly filed bill. Mr. Rogers of Wakefield, a neighboring town to Ossipee, disagreed with Winant and Nelson, stating the death penalty was a deterrent for homicides, citing that in twenty-five years only two men had been hanged out of forty-nine convictions. Then Rogers referred to the Frederick Small conviction, stating that in this instance, "a just verdict had been returned."[11]

Finally, Major Brennan of Peterborough declared that the decision of whether or not to institute the provision of capital punishment should be determined on a case by case basis. The option should be left in place for judges and juries to act on. Following Brennan's speech, a vote was taken and the bill was defeated, 190 to 142. Even if this bill had passed, it was doubtful that it would have had any effect on the sentence imposed upon Frederick Small, since his conviction was legally documented some three months before this legislation would have been passed into law. However, there was always the hope the governor would have commuted Small's sentence on the basis of this new law, if it had passed, although he was not duty-bound to do so.

Just when all expectation of a legal remedy had been dashed, Frederick Small was handed a new hope. With only five days remaining before Small's execution, Small's attorneys became aware of a possible infraction of the law by one of the jurors chosen to serve on the murder trial—Frank A. Whiting of Tamworth. A new complaint was issued on January 10, 1918 to the Superior Court which stated "Frederick L. Small's case became prejudiced by said Frank A. Whiting sitting upon his case as one of the twelve jurors, before whom he was tried; by reason of all which he did not have that fair, impartial trial to which he was entitled under the laws of the State of New Hampshire."[12]

Apparently, it had come to the attention of Small's defense lawyers that about three weeks after Frank Whiting returned home to Tamworth from the trial, he went to a horse-trot at White's Pond, which was about three miles from where he lived. At the trot, the murder case was mentioned by several people, and just about everyone was commending Whiting for choosing a just verdict. There was one man, however, who took opposition to the verdict and told Whiting he had no business condemning Frederick Small to death. Whiting then, according to several eyewitnesses, stated, "My mind was made up before I went down there that Small was guilty. And I never changed my mind one mite through the trial."[13] After receiving word of this infraction of New Hampshire state law, Sidney Stevens immediately filed an affidavit to request a new trial on behalf of his client. At last, it seemed Frederick Small's life might have been spared.

Small had not given up hope he would one day be exonerated from the conviction, and it would appear that his optimism was well placed. However, Judge Kivel, who happened to sit on the Superior Court, was called upon to make a ruling on the affidavit, and immediately requested that Frank A. Whiting produce a sworn statement as to his side of the story. In response, Frank Whiting swore before Fred Howell, the Justice of the Peace, "Upon examination by the court and counsel, I stated that I had a certain opinion in regard to the merits of the case; that if I was selected as a juror I should endeavor to lay aside that opinion and should do my duty as a juror; that if I sat in the trial I should endeavor to be fair both to the State and the respondent . . . . I did lay aside any opinion that I had and I did listen to all of the evidence with an open and unprejudiced mind and should have voted for an acquittal if I had heard any evidence that would have warranted me in so doing . . . . I carefully reviewed in my mind everything that had been presented and my judgment was that upon all of the facts as they then lay in my mind it seemed to me to be my plain duty under the oath I had taken to vote for a verdict of guilty with capital punishment."[14] Whiting further stated that he voted this way with much reluctance. He was searching for some reliable evidence that could have justified finding Frederick Small not guilty of the crime of which he was charged. But unfortunately, according to Whiting, there was no such evidence presented, and he had to vote his conscience. In reference to his confrontation with George Tasker at the horse-trot about the verdict, Whiting swore his exact words to Tasker were, "From the evidence I heard I knew he was guilty and you know it too."[15] Whiting totally denied stating that his mind was made up before the trial.

Once again Small's hopes were dashed. Attorney General Tuttle fought the very idea of considering a new trial for Frederick Small so close to the day of his scheduled execution. Tuttle stated this was a mere "by-play on justice"[16] and threatened he would strongly object to the consideration of this testimony by the court under such circumstances. Therefore, Small's plea for a new trial was dismissed by Chief Justice Kivel, and his execution was not stayed.

On January 14, 1918, Sheriff Chandler boarded a train for the journey to the Concord State Prison. For many involved in the trial, this trip would hold a sense of closure, that Florence Small's murder was finally avenged, and this evil man would no longer be a threat to society. But for Chandler, this journey had to have been a difficult one, for he was assigned to throw the switch, springing the trap door on which Frederick Small

X. QUESTIONS AND RESOLUTIONS

would be standing with a noose around his neck. As the top official in Carroll County, this obligation rested on the sheriff.

For the remainder of the train ride, Chandler sat quietly, gazing out the window at the passing landscape, much as Frederick Small had done when he took the same journey. When he arrived at the station in Concord, he was greeted with the news that Sidney Stevens was in a meeting with New Hampshire's Governor Keyes at that very moment, attempting to arrange a stay of execution. Because this meeting was still in session at 6:00 that evening, Chandler decided that it would be best to tour the death-room facility, on the chance the execution would still take place.

The death chamber was similar to the one used for the execution of convicted murderer Oscar J. Comery two years earlier. No gallows had been built. Instead, a cellar area was designed with a room directly above it where Small would be led for the carrying out of his execution. Sheriff Chandler walked over to the dangling rope, which measured 5/8 of an inch thick, and gave it a tug. Then he asked officials if the rope had been tested, because hanging ropes had a tendency to stretch when heavy weight was applied to them. The jail officials told the sheriff the rope had been tested periodically for the last ten days, and had stretched about ten inches. Satisfied the rope had stretched enough, Chandler inspected the 3 1/2 square foot trap door in the floor. He then checked the prisoner's data sheet, to ascertain Small's precise height. Finding that Small was five foot seven inches tall, Sheriff Chandler made his way to the basement, to measure the height of the cellar chamber. It would be a miscarriage of justice to have Small's body fall to the chamber below, only to be stopped suddenly upon impact with the basement floor. There was no chance of this happening however, for the ceiling of the cellar chamber was at least eight feet high. Even with a slight additional stretching of the rope, there appeared to be leeway of at least two feet. Once the task of inspecting the death chamber had been completed, Chandler, as well as many of the people who had been asked to witness the execution, filed into the prison cafeteria to hear the prison band perform for the other inmates. This was part of the regular routine for the Concord prison, and went on uninterrupted, although Small was not given permission to attend.

At 6:15, Frederick Small ate what was possibly going to be his last meal, since he still hadn't obtained word as to whether his defense council had been successful in gaining a stay of execution on his behalf. Small ate at the officers' table a meal that consisted of bread and butter, cold meat, prune juice, and a glass of milk. This meal was identical to what the other inmates were served that evening. Small didn't waste a single bite, and following dinner, he showered, shaved, and dressed in a brand new black suit with a blue and white striped shirt, which had no collar.

Small paced back and forth in his cell, as he awaited word from his attorneys about having his sentence commuted. At about 8:30 that evening, Small's attorney, Sidney Stevens, called to inform him that as hard as they had tried, they were unable to convince Governor Keyes to commute his sentence. Small's response to this news was as if it had been expected and he made a brief statement saying, "The only thing I can say is that I am resigned. God's will be done." [17] The pacing had ceased, and Small resolved himself to the fact that he had very little time left to live. Apart from the farewell meeting Small had with his brother, Frank, at about 10:00 that evening, these were the last words that prison officials ever heard Frederick Small speak.

At 10:15 P.M., Small was transferred from his cell, where he had spent the last eighteen days in silence, to the detention room next to the death chamber. This detention room was completely surrounded by flour bags piled high on all sides. Shortly thereafter, Small's spiritual minister, William F. Stevens, of the First Scientists Church in Concord, spent time with him. But Small had finished speaking, and no matter how hard Stevens persisted, Small would not say another word.

The twenty-nine spectators who had come to witness the execution of Frederick Small, were escorted into the death chamber at 12:05 A.M. This witness list included many people from the Ossipee area, including Dr. Hodsdon and Frank Ferrin. Because of the large number of witnesses, the room became filled to capacity, and the spectators spilled out into the adjoining corridor. The twelve men of the jury who voted to execute Small were seated with the medical officials in the cellar room. When all witnesses were settled, the warden approached Small's detention room, and walked inside.

"It's time," Warden Rowe said to the inmate, then turned to follow behind the sheriff, who led the procession to the death chamber. It was 12:14 A.M. Small made his way in the death procession, through a narrow hallway which led to the bakery, then up three steps and through another room overflowing with witnesses. When Small began his journey to the death chamber, he had a slight grin on his face. This expression quickly changed to astonishment, as he moved past the silent, expressionless men who watched him as he passed by, so closely he couldn't help but touch their arms as he advanced. Although Small's face had turned white, he kept a steady pace, never faltering, although his deformed right leg interrupted the silence with a conspicuous beat. Small hadn't anticipated seeing so many people he recognized, and as he entered the death chamber, he bowed to the spectators, who may have noticed something different about Small's appearance. That evening, he had shaved his mustache.

As they gathered in the death chamber, Chandler read the death warrant and Rev. William Stevens read a few words of encouragement. Then the guards placed four straps around Small's body, one securing his arms to his sides, another securing his wrists, the third holding his thighs together, and the final strap restraining his ankles. Some final words were read by Stevens as a hood was placed over Small's head, and the noose was secured around his neck. When all of the preparations had been made, Chandler stepped on the spring to release the trap door, at which time, the lights were diminished. It was 12:18 A.M. Nobody moved. For those few minutes, the only sound heard was the creaking of the rope as it swayed back and forth on its iron hook.

When the lights were turned on again, the jurors saw before them the lifeless body of Frederick L. Small, still swaying on the rope. At 12:27 A.M., Small's body was cut down, and he was pronounced dead by the medical personnel in attendance. A newspaper printed in Wolfeboro, New Hampshire, wrote of the hanging, "If Mr. Small did what his peers say he did and after the most searching examination, why should he not pay such penalty as the majority of his citizens consider their best safe-guard. This is not intimating that hanging is the best, nevertheless it is considered by New Hampshire people to be the most humane way to rid society of such undesirable citizens for the best protection of all."[18]

The body of Frederick Small was remanded to his brother, Frank, who arranged for its cremation. Frank's intent was to return home to Portland, Maine, with Frederick's ashes, where he would attend to his brother's burial. Frank also took possession of all of Frederick's worldly goods, which included the stove recovered from the ruins of the cottage. Although the state expressed an interest in keeping the stove, since a museum in the area wished to use it as part of an exhibit, Frank Small would hear nothing of it. Thus, arrangements were made for the stove to accompany Frank to Portland.

But Florence Curry Small wasn't as fortunate in securing distance between herself and the town where she had moved against her will so many years earlier. Although it was a beautiful, tranquil escape for the seasonal residents, for Florence, the town of Ossipee had brought forth feelings of loneliness and abuse unlike anything she had known before. A part of her would always remain in the earth under the lonesome little cottage, surrounded by the fieldstone foundation, which would entomb her ashes, trapping her there for all eternity.

x. QUESTIONS AND RESOLUTIONS

1 The State of New Hampshire Superior Court, *State Vs. Frederick Small: Respondent's Bill of Exceptions*, Carroll County Courthouse, December Term, pg. 19.

2 Ibid., pg. 19.

3 Ibid., pg. 20.

4 Ibid., pg. 23-24.

5 Ibid., pg. 19.

6 Ibid., pg. 19.

7 Ibid., pg. 25.

8 Reference to *The Wizard of Oz*.

9 "House Decides on April 12 as End of Session," *The Manchester Union Leader*, March 21, 1917, pg. 9.

10 "Legislative Edition: Penalty of Death," *Concord Evening Monitor*, March 20, 1917, pg. 1.

11 "House Decides on April 12 as End of Session," *The Manchester Union Leader*, March 21, 1917,   pg. 9.

12 *Letter from Frederick L. Small to the Honorable Judge Kivel, Chief Justice of the Superior Court, Requesting a New Trial*, Carroll County Courthouse, Jan 10, 1918, pg. 1.

13 Ibid., pg. 2.

14 *Sworn Statement of Frank A. Whiting*, Carroll County Courthouse, Jan. 9, 1918.

15 Ibid., pg. 2.

[16] *Letter from Attorney General Tuttle to Hon. William S. Matthews & Sidney F. Stevens, Esq., concerning their application to the Court for a new trial*, Carroll County Courthouse, Jan. 8, 1918,   pg. 1.

[17] "Broker Small Pays Extreme Penalty For Murder of Wife," *The Manchester Leader and Evening Union*, Jan. 15, 1918, pg. 11.

[18] "Pays Penalty," *The Granite State News*, Jan. 19, 1918, pg. 1.

XI. EPILOGUE

As the tragic story of Frederick and Florence Small came to its close, one would think that perhaps the sad history of the ill-fated cottage might have been put to rest as well. For with the departure of Frederick Small from their village, the citizens of Ossipee sought to erase the entire incident from their community. Although many may have been concerned that Frederick Small would become some kind of infamous folk hero to visitors in the area, the fact was that life went on in an ordinary fashion, and the Small murder trial was scarcely, if ever, discussed. Folks simply wanted to forget about the crime committed by the out-of-state man, verifying their opinion that although outsiders viewed the Ossipee locals with suspicion, truly they were the ones who needed a watchful eye. However, those who lived through the crime and trial would never be able to forget its impact on the innocence of the tiny village, and although seldom mentioned, the memory lingers to this day as if it had taken place just yesterday. This fact has been exemplified by Mark Winkley III, grandson to the famous mason. Mr. Winkley was merely four years old at the time of the incident, yet was able to clearly recollect many details of this dire event in the history of Ossipee. Although in his eighties now, Mr. Winkley remembered his grandfather's insistence that he could have fixed the leak in the fieldstone foundation, if Frederick Small had been willing to pay for a cement floor in his basement. Mr. Winkley's recollection of details was extraordinary.

Furthermore, when Anna Foley walked into the general store and encountered some Ossipee natives in 1955, there was immediate recognition of the address of the incident by all who heard where she had taken up residency. For although the cottage appeared to have been lost that evening on September 28, 1916, the passage of time combined with the attraction of a great deal on a prime piece of lakefront property, served to make this cottage destined to rise again from the ashes.

On January 16, 1918, records show that Small's attorneys, Matthews and Stevens, took possession of the ill-fated lakefront property. However, it wasn't long before Stevens and Matthews remanded the property to the town of Ossipee in an attempt to cover some back taxes owed. Thus, on February 21, 1922, the town of Ossipee took possession of the real estate formerly owned by Frederick and Florence Small. But in 1954, the property was purchased from the town by a woman named Barbara Allen for a ridiculously low price, which basically settled up the accrued taxes owed. However, in less than a year, Ms. Allen sold the property, which included a lakefront cottage, to Anna's husband, Joe Foley. Therefore, some time after the hanging of Frederick Small the cottage was rebuilt, using mostly new materials with one exception—the fieldstone foundation which was unharmed by the fire and was functional to support a new structure. The builder opted to save some money and add a little charm to the new dwelling by basing its framework on the existing fieldstone foundation.

This story interested me because although I have no memory of the cottage or any of the events that took place inside it that night, I was one of the occupants of the cottage described in the first chapter. My role was merely as an observer, a fifteen-month-old baby whose parents had chosen to vacation at Lake Ossipee in August 1956. Throughout my childhood, when different relatives on my father's side would come over for a visit, the story of the "haunting" would inevitably be retold as supper dishes were stacked for washing and twilight approached.

Everyone admits my parents had no prior knowledge that anything out of the ordinary took place at the site of the cottage, which is an important point. For if anything had been known about its tragic history, it would have been easy to explain the incident as the work of an overactive imagination. And my parents were the last people in the world to have overactive imaginations. They were both hardworking, honest people who were not at all superstitious. The fact that my parents would swear by this story made it so intriguing. They believed nothing beyond what could be proven, which is why for a while, they must have felt very strange about what had taken place in the cottage that night, and wanted nothing more than to deny its ever happening and get on with their lives. That is, until by chance, they found their proof.

One cold February morning in the late 1950's, after returning from church, my father sat down in his favorite chair to read the Boston Sunday paper while my mom started dinner. This particular paper contained a reprint of an article which had originally appeared in *The American* on February 21, 1936, as part of a popular detective series. "The American Crime at Ossipee"[1] was the original heading of Frank McLean's story. The word "Ossipee" immediately caught my father's eye. As he read on, my father began to realize that this cottage described in the article could have been built on the same lot as his mother's cottage. By this time, his mother and stepfather had sold the cottage to my uncle. Consequently, my father felt free to call Joe Foley. Much to his surprise, my father learned that both Anna and Joe knew of the events that took place in their former cottage, and never told him about them. The cottage was the topic of dinner conversation that day, and because my parents' fears had been validated by historical evidence, the topic of the haunting was no longer considered taboo.

Although my family's stories of the haunting remained unaltered with the passage of time, the story of the murder itself had become somewhat changed. Having read the newspaper article years before, neither my father nor my grandparents could remember the name of the "hideous looking hunchback", the truly "ugly, crippled man whose main view was that of the ground." My father's description of Frederick Small got more grotesque with each retelling of the story. And according to my father, one day, for no apparent reason other than shear meanness, this despicable character decided to kill his wife, set his house on fire, and hop a ride to Boston for an alibi.

In my father's recollection of the story, the murder occurred somewhat differently, too. The miserable wretch of a husband strung his wife up with a noose around her neck, using one of the attic rafters to support the rope. Then he set a slow burning fire and exited the house quickly, yelling "good-bye, dear" as he left, so it would appear his wife was still alive. When the fire really began to get going, it burned through the rope before it burned the woman's body, sending the body plunging into the basement, which was flooded with water; because that cellar was always flooded with water. Nobody discovered the body until spring, since it was frozen all winter long when the water in the cellar had turned to ice. But in the spring, when the water thawed and the seasonal residents began to return to the region and open their cottages for the summer, the poor wife's body was discovered in the burned out cottage, lying preserved in the icy water, with the noose still around her neck. This is when the manhunt ensued, trying to track down the husband who had left the area, presuming he had literally gotten away with murder. We never knew whether the husband was caught, and this lack of information didn't seem to detract from the essence of the story. After all, if this story was ever thoroughly analyzed, serious flaws could be found, leading one to doubt the validity of the entire tale. However, although the retelling of the tale of the murder was sketchy, the essence of the stories of the haunting were never altered, and always appeared credible, which led me to search for the true story behind the haunting.

After researching the truth about the cottage's history, the sole remaining question would appear to be, whose presence was felt on that fateful night in August 1956? According to my father, it was the wife's spirit, having died in such a vile manner at the cruel hand of her grotesque husband. And perhaps it was Mrs. Small. Although her life didn't end exactly as the story had been told throughout the years; if anything, her true death was even more horrific. Furthermore, nobody ever agreed that all of Florence Small's remains had been recovered from the basement. It was highly possible that some of Florence's ashes could still have rested inside the confines of the cottage cellar. After all, the fieldstone foundation into which her body dropped still remained at the time of the haunting.

However, Florence Small's death had been avenged by the conviction and hanging of her husband, if he really did commit the murder, and thus in the end, she received justice. This outcome should have put her mind at ease and her body at rest, allowing Florence to continue on to wherever it is that peaceful spirits go when their cause has been served, thus leaving the spirit of Frederick Small as a possible haunting specter. Perhaps Frederick didn't commit the murder. Perhaps a tramp really did come into the home of Florence Small that evening, as Frederick vehemently insisted. Or perhaps one of the many men who Small angered in the course of his lifetime, which was quite a ponderous list, came to the cottage prepared to kill Frederick and Florence, and rig a device to set the cottage on fire some hours after he was out of the area, destroying the evidence. When he found that Frederick was gone to Boston, he decided to carry out the murder of Frederick's wife, and frame Frederick as the mastermind. This plausible theory was never considered by counsel for the defense or the prosecution. Possibly, Frederick can't rest until his reputation has been restored.

Or perhaps there was simply an unrest on that piece of property that wouldn't disappear with the passage of time. When attending my grandmother's funeral two summers ago, I asked my uncle if anything strange had happened at the cottage while he owned it.

"Well, I know a terrible murder happened at that cottage," he replied. When I told him that I knew about the murder, he looked at me somewhat puzzled and said, "You mean, something spiritual?" I eagerly awaited his reply.

"Let's see," he began, looking up at the ceiling for a moment. "The only thing truly momentous that I remember happening in that cottage was when a friend and I went up to the house for the weekend, and the entire septic system erupted. We spent the whole weekend digging out. Now that's an experience you just don't easily forget. It was right after that I sold the place. I'd had enough of the old cottage," my uncle concluded.

I looked at my brother and his wife, and then at my husband, all seated at our table. We all laughed and decided that my uncle was as gifted in the art of storytelling as my father. When my uncle had left, my sister-in-law explained that she had heard that sometimes apparitions will not appear to people who are not predisposed to accepting their existence. We all nodded and agreed she was probably right.

The concern that Frederick Small would be remembered for all eternity was no real threat, since nobody could recall his name when I first visited the Ossipee Historical Society several years ago, specifically inquiring about the event. The woman who headed the historical society at the time was very helpful, however she hadn't been a long-time resident of Ossipee. Still, she remembered reading an article about a murder that happened out by the lake during the time period which I had indicated, but she couldn't recall many of the details. She thought the man's name was Smart, perhaps confusing it with the Pamela Smart murder case of a few years ago, where a New Hampshire teacher allegedly commissioned one of her students to kill her husband. However, this gracious lady was able to locate a one-page article concerning the murder. Although not weighty in details, this article provided me with the names of the victim and the murderer, as well as the dates of the incident and of the trial. With this information, I was able to contact the Carroll County Courthouse and ask that the records of the trial be recovered from the building's basement archives. Amazingly, much of the information was still intact and the staff at the courthouse was somewhat intrigued by the request. It was difficult to determine whether their curiosity was peaked by the case itself, or by the fact that someone was interested in researching a case that was clearly almost 100 years old.

One clerk noted that she was reading some of the records to make sure she'd found everything I had requested. Then she looked up at me and said, "This man really wanted to be sure his wife was dead, didn't he?"

Another member of the courthouse staff observed, "They didn't fool around back then, did they? He was convicted and hung within a little over a year!"

For whatever their reason, the interest of the courthouse staff in this case only served to encourage me to investigate further. After contacting *The Boston Globe* and the State Library in Concord, New Hampshire, I was able to piece together the entire story with reliable accuracy. I was intrigued not only by the story itself, but by the way people lived and thought at the turn of the century, when World War I was raging in Europe.

After returning to Ossipee once again to take a look at some old pictures in the Ossipee library, I had a chance meeting with the new President of the Ossipee Historical Society, Barry Hill. Although he had recently moved to Ossipee from Sudbury, Massachusetts, he had a great deal of knowledge about the history and trends in the town of Ossipee itself. He also noted that the Mountainview railway, which often served Frederick Small and other residents of the community, had become the Chat and Chew eatery we had passed on the way to the historical society's building. Although Mr. Hill was familiar with the Small murder and subsequent trial, he recommended that I speak with Mark Winkley, the grandson of the well respected mason by the same name. Mr. Hill remarked that Mr. Winkley was beginning to have a little trouble getting around, but his mind was still sharp. Mr. Hill was right about that. The historical society often referred inquiries to Mr. Winkley when they weren't able to find information on a specific topic themselves.

Over the course of that summer, Barry Hill played an invaluable part in complimenting my research. He had located many old black and white pictures of the town as it was back in Small's day, and couldn't believe his good fortune when a long-time resident of the community cleaned out his attic and found an old snapshot of Frederick Small crossing the street in Center Ossipee accompanied by George Philbrick, Fred Bean, and another unidentified man, to attend his arraignment in the old Chamberlain Hall. It seemed that for a time, everywhere Barry Hill would go to locate information concerning an unrelated topic he was researching, he would stumble over something referring to the Small case, which he would graciously forward to me. Barry Hill's greatest discovery, however, was a book written by a former sheriff of Carroll County, James Welch, which contained an entire chapter on his experience as a juror in the Frederick Small murder trial. This was a breakthrough in being able to gain some insight into the minds of the jurors before, during, and immediately following the trial. For some reason, the jurors made a pact among themselves not to talk about their deliberations, which left the media with little information as to how they made their decision. In writing his memoirs, James Welch gave us this insight, which greatly enhanced this story.

Following up, I sent a list of names of other key players in the Small murder case to Jane Lyman, a researcher at the Concord State Library, another invaluable resource for tapping into information which was important to understanding this story. I was hoping to uncover a collection of memoirs written by another juror, a lawyer, or a witness in the trial. This effort was to no avail. James Welch appeared to be the only one who put his recollections in print. With most everybody connected to this murder case long since deceased, memoirs and court records were my primary sources for first-hand information concerning the whole matter.

A visit to the Carroll County Registry of Deeds in Ossipee provided me with information concerning the ownership of the property throughout the years. Because my family's accounts of the murder had been embellished and altered with each storytelling, I became suspect that it was possible my father or step-grandfather could have been mistaken about the ownership of the property. Perhaps the tract of land purchased by my grandfather wasn't actually the same land where the murder had occurred. After researching the truth about what had happened at that site, in a strange way, I secretly hoped it had all been a mistake. However, after tracing the deed which Frederick Small signed, I found it to be identical to the deed belonging to Joe Foley. The spotted poplar tree and the iron pipe cited on the deed as boundaries for the property matched on both deeds, and as I read on, an eerie picture sprang to my mind of Joe Foley and Frederick Small, simultaneously signing his name to the exact same document in front of me. It was then that I realized the story was all true, that the land was precisely the same. And I had to wonder if my grandfather had paused to hear a detailed account of what had taken place on that tract of land, or had been privy to seeing the exact replica of what he was about to sign, with Frederick Small's signature on it, if it would have swayed him at all in buying the property. It is interesting to note that although newspaper accounts of the value of Small's lakefront property was about $900, the deed stated that Frederick Small paid $1.00 and other considerations for his lakeside home.

When first deciding to write this book, I took my mother for a ride up to Ossipee to see if she could recognize the cottage where she had spent an unsettling evening about forty-five years ago. I wanted to get a feel for the area and the cottage, since all I could remember about the Ossipee region was a wonderful pine scent that filled the air, and a little garter snake my mother accidentally set me down beside when I was a toddler. I remember delighting in its wiggling across my feet, trying to escape under the stairway. Of the cottages themselves, I had no real memory.

My mother recognized the old cottage with no hesitation, and pointed out many of the surrounding cottages, giving their owners' names at the time when she summered in the area so many years before. Although this account is totally factual, I did not reveal the true address of the cottage in the interest of preserving the current owner's privacy.

It wasn't until this book was published and selling in bookstores that I became aware of the most recent history of the cottage. One dreary Saturday morning, the local bookstore called to tell me that there was a man buying every copy of the book that she had in stock. She said that he claimed to be the current owner of the cottage, and he was buying the copies to give to family and friends. The storeowner explained that after speaking with the man for a while, she mentioned that she knew my phone number and asked if he would like to speak to me. The man eagerly accepted the offer.

It was my good fortune to be home that morning, because I really wanted to know if anyone other than my parents had a strange experience in the old cottage. What I learned fascinated me, because although I believed my parents' stories, I found it odd that their claim had not been substantiated by anyone else in all these years.

The man introduced himself as the son of the man who bought the cottage from my uncle so many years earlier. The cottage had remained in his family for forty-odd years. After the stories I had heard about the old place, I couldn't imagine anyone holding onto the cottage for that long. I always thought of it as a cursed piece of property.

Immediately, I thought to myself, "The cottage must not be haunted. His family wouldn't have stayed all this time if it was."

After some small talk, I finally got up the nerve to ask the caller the same question I had asked my uncle several years ago, anticipating a similar reply.

"Over the years, did you ever notice anything strange happening in the cottage?" I asked.

The man's matter-of-fact answer went something like this. "Oh the cottage is definitely haunted. We've seen evidence of this many times throughout the years."

"In what way?" I asked, not anticipating this response and a little jealous that my family hadn't held on to the cottage, allowing me to experience the phenomenon for myself.

"Oh, subtle things," he replied. "Occasionally we would hear footsteps, or things wouldn't be where you left them, or lights would turn on and off for no good reason."

"Really," I said. "Who do you think is haunting the cottage?"

"We think it's the wife," he said.

"My parents always thought it was Florence haunting the cottage, too." I reminisced.

"But there is something interesting about this spirit," the caller continued. "She only shows her presence when the cottage is practically empty. If there are a lot of people around, we don't know she's there."

"That would explain why my parents were the only ones in my family who experienced her presence. Most of the time there were many people in the cottage." I said.

We exchanged phone numbers and said our goodbyes, and I immediately called my parents to tell them that they weren't the only ones who thought the cottage was haunted.

The cottage has changed little since the day my uncle sold it. The basement still leaks, although countless attempts have been made to keep the spring water out. The curse of the antiquated fieldstone foundation, which was never really watertight, seems to be in full force to this day, with Florence Arlene Curry Small keeping a watchful eye over all who enter the little cottage with the picturesque mountain view.

1 McLean, pg. 1.

Florence Small

Frederick Small

James Welch, juror in
the Small trial and later,
Sheriff of Carroll County.

Deputy Sheriff George Philbrick
(left) & Frederick Small (right)

Joe & Ann Foley, owners of the
Small's cottage in the 1950's.

Steve and Thelma's two children, Ron & Jan (six and four
years old), at a different cottage on Ossipee Lake.

The jurors selected for the Small murder trial.

Investigators and volunteers search the Small cottage cellar
following the tragic fire.

PHOTO GALLERY
Places

The Central House, where Frederick Small stayed after his cottage burned.

Carroll County Courthouse, where Frederick Small's murder trial was the first trial to be held in this new courthouse.

Center Ossipee, New Hampshire: This photo shows the railway station that Frederick Small left from on his trip to Boston the day his cottage caught fire.

The jury room for the Small trial.

An original juror's chair.

Judge Kivel (top left), inside the courtroom for the Small murder trial.

1 2 3 4.

Smalls hearing

1. Fred Bean 2 not known
3. Small 4 Geo. Philbrick

This photo depicting Small walking towards Chamberlain Hall to attend his hearing was taken by an Ossipee resident, who later wrote down the names of the people he recognized.

BIBLIOGRAPHY

Books:

Dodge, Timothy, *Crime and Punishment in New Hampshire, 1812-1914, Volume I,* Dissertation, Durham, NH: University of New Hampshire, 1992.

Harkness, Marjorie Gane, and Lilian C. McGrew, *High Sheriff: Being the Reminiscences of James Welch, Former Sheriff of Carroll County, New Hampshire.* Tamworth, New Hampshire: Tamworth Historical Society, 1960.

Squires, James Duane, *The Granite State of The United States: A History of New Hampshire from 1623 to the Present, Volume 1,* New York: The American Historical Company, 1956.

Ossipee New Hampshire, 1785-1985: The Age of Promise, 1820 -1860, Ossipee, New Hampshire: Ossipee Historical Society.

Court Documents:

Inventory of Articles Found by Sheriff Arthur W. Chandler in the Traveling Bag of Frederick L. Small at Mountainview, Ossipee, Carroll County Courthouse, Sept. 29, 1916.

A Listing of State and Defendant's Exhibits, Carroll County Courthouse, Dec. 1916 & Jan. 1917.

Superior Court Grand Jury Indictment Against Frederick L. Small, Carroll County Courthouse, Dec. 1, 1916.

The State of New Hampshire Superior Court, *State Vs. Frederick Small: Respondent's Bill of Exceptions,* Carroll County Courthouse, December Term, 1916.

A True Copy of the Examination of Frank A. Whiting as a Juror in State v. Frederick L. Small, Carroll County Courthouse, Jan. 8, 1918.

Letter from Attorney General Tuttle to Hon. William S. Matthews & Sidney F. Stevens, Esq. concerning their application to the Court for a new trial, Carroll County Courthouse, Jan. 8, 1918.

Sworn Statement of Frank A. Whiting, Carroll County Courthouse, Jan. 9, 1918.

Letter from Frederick L. Small to the Honorable Judge Kivel, Chief Justice of the Superior Court, requesting a new trial, Carroll County Courthouse, Jan. 10, 1918.

Newspapers:

"Wife's Affections Valued at $500,000." *The New York Times,* New York, NY, February 10, 1909.

"Soden Must Pay $10,000," *The New York Times,* New York, NY, April 28, 1911.

"Small to Face Charge of Murder in First Degree," *The Manchester Union*, Manchester, NH, Sept. 30, 1916.

"Resin is Placed on Woman's Body," *The Manchester Union*, Manchester, NH, Oct. 2, 1916.

"Empty Shells Found in Ruins," *The Manchester Union*, Manchester, NH, Oct. 3, 1916.

"Six Witnesses to Testify for Small Defense," *The Manchester Union*, Manchester, NH, Oct. 5, 1916.

"State Arrays Its Evidence Against Small," *The Manchester Union*, Manchester, NH, Oct. 6, 1916.

"New Autopsy on Mrs. Small's Body," *The Manchester Union*, Manchester, NH, Oct. 7, 1916.

"Murder Charged: Fred L. Small Suspected as Guilty Party," *The Granite State News*, Wolfboro, NH, Oct. 17, 1916.

"Court Doings: Grand Jury Report Finding Four Indictments," *The Granite State News*, Wolfboro, NH, Dec. 9, 1916.

"Court Doings: Small Amount of Business This Term - Four Divorces Granted - List of Jurors Drawn for the Small Murder Trail - Notes," *The Granite State News*, Wolfboro, NH, Dec. 16, 1916.

"Charge of Wife Murder: Faced by Small in the Carroll County Superior Court," *Concord Evening Monitor*, Concord, NH, Dec. 26, 1916.

"Charest's Skeleton Found, Mystery Finally Solved," *Manchester Union Leader*, Manchester, NH, Dec. 26, 1916.

"Small's Trial Begins Today," *Manchester Union Leader*, Manchester, NH, Dec. 26, 1916.

"Small Jury is Complete, Trial Now Under Way," *The Manchester Leader and Evening Union*, Manchester, NH, Dec. 27, 1916.

"The Jury Completed: Twelve Men Selected for Trial at Ossipee of Frederick L. Small," *Concord Evening Monitor*, Concord, NH, Dec. 27, 1916.

"Declares Small Had Threatened to Murder Wife," *The Manchester Leader and Evening Union*, Manchester, NH, Dec. 28, 1916.

"Small Had Made Threats," *Concord Evening Monitor*, Concord, NH, Dec. 28, 1916.

"Chase Describes Small's Interest in Joint Policy," *The Manchester Leader and Evening Union*, Manchester, NH, Dec. 29, 1916.

"Had Heavy Insurance," *Concord Evening Monitor*, Concord, NH, Dec. 29, 1916.

"Inventory Discussed, Revolver Is Identified," *Concord Evening Monitor*, Concord, NH, Dec. 30, 1916.

"Murder Hearing: F. L. Small Charged with Killing His Wife," *The Granite State News*, Wolfboro, NH, Dec. 30, 1916.

"Sad Termination," *The Granite State News*, Wolfboro, NH, Dec. 30, 1916.

"Small's Inventory Made No Mention of Jewelry," *The Manchester Leader and Evening Union*, Manchester, NH, Dec. 30, 1916.

"Small Likely to Take Stand in Own Behalf," *The Manchester Union*, Manchester, NH, Jan. 1, 1917.

"Woman Was Strangled," *Concord Evening Monitor*, Concord, NH, Jan. 1, 1917.

"Court Puts Ban on Contents of Laura's Letters," *The Manchester Leader and Evening Union*, Manchester, NH, Jan. 2, 1917.

"Importance in Hours of Meals," *Concord Evening Monitor*, Concord, NH, Jan. 2, 1917.

"Direct Case Against Small Nears Completion," *The Manchester Leader and Evening Union*, Manchester, NH, Jan. 3, 1917.

"The Setting of the Fire," *Concord Evening Monitor*, Concord, NH, Jan. 3, 1917.

"Head of Murder Victim on View in Court Room," *The Manchester Leader and Evening Union*, Manchester, NH, Jan. 4, 1917.

"The Device of an Incendiary," *Concord Evening Monitor*, Concord, NH, Jan. 4, 1917.

"The Great Event of Inauguration at the State House," *Concord Evening Monitor*, Concord, NH, Jan. 4, 1917.

"Denies Motion for Acquittal," *Concord Evening Monitor*, Concord, NH, Jan. 5, 1917.

"General Denial is Defense of Broker Small," *The Manchester Leader and Evening Union*, Manchester, NH, Jan. 5, 1917.

"Governor's Ball Was Brilliant," *Concord Evening Monitor*, Concord, NH, Jan. 5, 1917.

"Door in Small Cottage Locked From Inside," *The Manchester Leader and*

Evening Union, Manchester, NH, Jan. 6, 1917.

"Locked on the Inside," *Concord Evening Monitor,* Concord, NH, Jan. 6, 1917.

"The Small Trial," *The Granite State News,* Wolfboro, NH, Jan. 6, 1917.

"Dr. Sarah A. Jenness: Brief Sketch of Her Useful Life and Tribute to Her Memory," *The Granite State News,* Wolfboro, NH, Jan. 6, 1917.

"Dr. Sarah A. Jenness," *The Granite State News,* Wolfboro, NH, Jan. 6, 1917.

"Arguments Presented," *Concord Evening Monitor,* Concord, NH, Jan. 8, 1917.

"Final Arguments in Small Murder Trial Are Begun," *The Manchester Leader and Evening Union,* Manchester, NH, Jan. 8, 1917.

"'I am Innocent,' Prisoner Cries Before Sentence," *The Manchester Leader and Evening Union,* Manchester, NH, Jan. 9, 1917.

"To Be Hanged on Jan. 15, 1918," *Concord Evening Monitor,* Concord, NH, Jan. 9, 1917.

"Small in the State Prison," *Concord Evening Monitor,* Concord, NH, Jan. 10, 1917.

"Small Passes Through City," *The Manchester Leader and Evening Union,* Manchester, NH, Jan. 10, 1917.

"Small Case," *The Granite State News,* Wolfboro, NH, Jan. 13, 1917.

"All Honor Given Today," *Concord Evening Monitor,* Concord, NH, Jan. 24, 1917.

"259 Bills Are Introduced in House Last Day," *The Manchester Union Leader,* Manchester, NH, Jan. 24, 1917.

"Legislative Edition: Penalty of Death," *Concord Evening Monitor,* Concord, NH, March 20, 1917.

"House Decides on April 12 as End of Session," *The Manchester Union Leader,* Manchester, NH, March 21, 1917.

"Broker Small Pays Extreme Penalty For Murder of Wife," *The Manchester Leader and Evening Union,* Manchester, NH, Jan. 15, 1918.

"Pays Penalty," *The Granite State News,* Wolfboro, NH, Jan. 19, 1918.

"Florence Small Slain In the 'Arson Engine Perfect Crime,'" The American, Boston, MA, Feb. 21, 1936.

"Ossipee Recalls: A Murder That Was Too Perfect," *Home Town History,* April 22, 1993.

Magazines:

Odlin, John W. "Two Gruesome Murders . . . One Solved: The Josie Lang-maid Murder," *Yankee*, Aug. 1940.

Pamphlets:

Hill, Barry. "A Terrible Fire," *Ossipee Almanac: Newsletter of the Ossipee Historical Society*, Fall 1998.

Laws:

Chapter 38. *"An Act to Punish Tramps,"* Sections 1-9, Approved by the Senate and House of Representatives in General Court, 1 August 1878.

Consultations:

John Hancock Mutual Life Insurance, Research Dept., Boston, Massachusetts, Dec. 1998.

www.ingramcontent.com/pod-product-compliance
Lightning Source LLC
Chambersburg PA
CBHW051903090426

42811CB00003B/438